MUSLIM HEROES OF THE WORLD

MUSLIM HEROES OF THE WORLD

by

M. Atiqul Haque

Taha Publishers

Published by: TaHa Publishers Ltd.
1 Wynne Road
London SW9 0BB
United Kingdom

Editing and Typesetting by Bookwork, Norwich

British Library Cataloguing in Publication Data
Haque, M. Atiqul
Muslim heroes of the world.
1. Short stories
I. Title

ISBN 0 907461 75 1

Printed and bound in Great Britain at Southampton Book Co., Southampton

Table of Contents

An Introduction

Muslim Heroes of the World is an attempt to present heroes and personalities of the Muslim World who have made a significant contribution to the rich treasurehouse of Islamic history and Islamic heritage. But since the subject is vast and the period is long I have had to be selective in my choice of personalities. I was also constrained to be selective by reason of the lack of sources. Islamic history books there are, but history books deal with events, and we were interested in people. The nature of this book demands the kind of complete portrait that is very rarely found in history books, so I had to grope in the darkness to find the necessary material. Most of the biographies I have used were written by Western writers, whose bias and prejudices against Islam have invariably coloured their writing.

At last I was lucky enough to come across a book of biography, written by a great man of our country, Justice Abdul Maudood. He will remain immortal in the minds of those readers who care about Islamic history and Muslim personalities. He took great pains to produce a book called *Muslim Manish*a which means "Muslim Heroes". My book *Muslim Heroes of the World* is, in fact, a copy of his great book *Muslim Manisha*.

It is a wonderful book and he had to do a lot of reading to collect the material for it, but nobody, it seems, has taken any notice of it, possibly, because it was written in Bengali, and also possibly, because he was not generally considered a writer as he was a Justice of the High Court of Pakistan. Anyway, his efforts have not gone in vain. I am completely indebted to him, and I will pray for him as will all those who read this book.

1
Muhammad, the Greatest Leader

Among His servants those who have knowledge fear Allah truly, for Allah is Exalted in Might and oft- forgiving (Qur'an 35:28)

Who can truly understand the creation of this universe and its inner significance? Only Allah's servants who know i.e. who have the inner knowledge which comes from acquaintance with the spiritual world. Those who know the spiritual world are the people who can appreciate Allah's creation and His management of this universe.

This appreciation brings the fearful awareness which is the hallmark of a truly knowledgeable person in this world in relation to his Lord. This knowledge of the spirit is what the Qur'an emphasizes in the passage quoted and it is repeated in several other places in various ways throughout the Qur'an. The Qur'an says, *"Are those who know and those who do not know the same?"* (Qur'an 39:9) And again, *"Are the blind and the sighted equal?"* (Qur'an 6:50) Here the blind are those who do not know and they are compared elsewhere to donkeys which carry the revealed Books but do not know what they are carrying. (Qur'an 62:5)

The sighted are those who are spiritually enlightened and who know who they are, the reason that they have come to this world and where they are going after they take leave of this world. They are the people who have surrendered to their Lord and who seek and take guidance from their Lord. They are Muslims.

The early Muslims were endowed with this spiritual knowledge, and most of the Khalifs, although they apparently led a life of pomp and grandeur, were extremely serious and religious people. And almost all of them were men of literature and patrons of knowledge and science. As Sir John Glubb said,

> Well-educated in both religion and literature, Caliph Haroon ar-Rashid was a patron of the learned and of the poets. He sought out the company of ascetics and of religious teachers on his visits to Mecca and Medina and would refer to them the religious difficulties which at times confronted him. He is said to have been much addicted to long prayers and used to weep when he heard a pious sermon. He was always extremely orthodox in his religious professions. He reign was an age of intellectual activity, particularly in the field of theology and religious jurisprudence.

Islam spread rapidly in a remarkably short time. How? This question has perplexed many and many people attribute a multitude of different reasons to this expansion. But they forget the basic fact that Islam is the religion of Allah and that Muhammad is His Prophet. From the very beginning of Islam this Prophet started,

> ...preaching the word of Allah, simultaneously establishing a community, a great society (*millat*) with a clear code of conduct, organisation and administration. This was the origin of the future glorious Islamic State in which the Qur'anic

> teachings and Muhammad's exemplification of them were to be the ushers in of Europe's Renaissance and the harbingers of the modern age of science.
> (*Islam: An Instrument of World Peace* by Choudhuri Nazir Ahmed Khan)

Again let us consider the historic speech of the Prophet on Mount Arafat which is now accepted as a great "Charter of Human Dignity".

It is recorded that on that eventful day the holy Prophet was riding his camel, Qaswah, whose reins were in the hands of Bilal, a freed slave, while another freed slave, Usama, was screening the Prophet's face from the ferocity of the midday sun. On that day several of his kith and kin must have longed to get the distinction of being his attendants, but the Prophet who was to usher in an era of justice and equality for mankind proclaimed:

> The Arab has no preference over the non-Arab and vice versa; neither birth nor rank determine a man's status, but only his piety and righteousness set the standard of his excellence.

Writing under the caption, "Who were History's Great Leaders," Jules Masserman, a famous U.S. psychoanalyst, says,

> Leaders must fulfil three functions: provide for the well-being of the led, provide a social organisation in which people feel relatively secure, and provide them with one set of beliefs. People like Pasteur and Salk are leaders in the

first sense; people like Gandhi and Confucius, on the one hand, Alexander, Caesar and Hitler, on the other, are leaders in the second or perhaps the third sense. Jesus and Buddha belong to the third category alone. Perhaps the greatest leader of all times was Muhammad who combined all the three functions. To a lesser degree Moses did the same. (*Time Magazine*, July, 1974)

2
The Victory of Makka

The Qur'an is indeed the Message for you and for your people and soon you shall all be brought to account.
(Qur'an 43:44)

> Muhammad the conqueror was not vindictive. A general amnesty was proclaimed . . . . Eight years before he had fled from Mecca under cover of darkness, and lain hidden three days in a cave on Mount Thor . . . . . Now ten thousand warriors were ready to obey his least command and his native town lay helpless at his feet. . . . Although he had himself been persecuted in the city and although many of his bitterest opponents were still living, he won all hearts by his clemency on his day of triumph. Such generosity, or statesmanship, was particularly remarkable among Arabs, a race to whom revenge has always been dear. His success had been won by policy and diplomacy rather than by military action.
> *The Great Arab Conquests* by Sir John Glubb

Islam, it is alleged, was spread by a "sword in one hand and the Qur'an in the other." This assertion is absolutely false and unfounded. Islam was spread by the beauty of its adherents. The Prophet Muhammad never asked any of his followers to accept the conversion of any man who had become a Muslim by coercion or force. On the contrary, several Khalifs and Kings of Islam discouraged large-scale conversions in view of the fact that they would be deprived of large sums of money on account of the *jizya* and *kharaj* which is paid by non-Muslims under Muslim rule.

The "sword in one hand and the Qur'an in the other " is a concoction and innovation of Western secularists to malign Islam as a religion of force and aggression. Is not it a fact that the thousands of Makkans who surrendered to the Prophet on his Victory march to Makka were pardoned unconditionally without requiring them to accept Islam. They were told "to remain in their houses and to close the door or to seek sanctuary in Abu Sufyan's house or in the square of the Ka'ba" and thus they would be safe.

On the day of the Treaty of Hudaybiyya, one of the Makkan emissaries, reporting back to the leaders of the Quraysh, gave a vivid sketch of the prestige of the Prophet among his followers:

> I have been to Chosroes in his Kingdom and I have seen Caesar and the Prince of Abyssinia among their subjects, but never have I seen a king among his people treated with such respect as Muhammad among his Companions.

> When we are perplexed to account for the sudden rise of Islam, we will do well to remember these few lines. The aura of the Prophet's personality cannot be recaptured by us. Yet there was doubtless something about him which inspired this utter devotion and which constituted one of the principal causes of the success of Islam. - Sir John Glubb

Thus we see the principal cause of the success of Islam

was not military action or the sword but the Prophet's character and personality. Just as the Prophet never asked his followers to accept forced conversion nor did he encourage blind faith. He asked his followers to spread the Message through learning and enlightenment as to the Truth. The Truth, he said, would be vivid and crystal clear, once the people were enable to "drink deep into the Qur'an." The Qur'an is the best book and the most authentic guide. He said: the contents of the Qur'an come under five headings:

> Things lawful, things unlawful, clear and positive precepts, mysteries and examples. Consider lawful that which is there declared to be so; and that which is forbidden as unlawful; obey the precepts, believe in the mysteries and take warning from the examples. (*Hadith*)

He also said, "An hour's contemplation is better than sixty years' adoration," and again, "Seek knowledge from the cradle to the grave."

Thus we see Islam did not spread through "the sword". It spread through knowledge and piety. All the great preachers of Islam who travelled unarmed and unharmed throughout the world and who succeeded in taking Islam to Africa, Asia, Europe, China, etc. were all great men of learning. They preached Islam by their character and conviction. Hundreds of dervishes and preachers like 'Abdu'l-Qadir al-Jilani, Khawaja Mu'inuddin Chishti, Nizamuddin Awlia, Hazrat Shah Jalal, Data Gani Shah, etc. were all men of learning and were great partrons of learning. And it is because of their learning and preaching that the Muslims of the Indian sub-continent now number so many millions.

In evaluating the rise of Islam we must remember two things: the Qur'an and the Prophet's character. When analysing the character of the Prophet we must remember that, although he was unlettered he laid full emphasis on knowledge and contemplation, which qualities form the basis of modern science. The Bedouins of Arabia drank deep into the Qur'an and the *Sunnah* and thus:

> In less than fifty years, the Bedouins of Arabia established the greatest empire in the world of their day, and one of the greatest in history.
> *The Sunday Telegraph.*

Thus education always played a major part in the policies of all the Muslim rulers in Cordoba and Granada, in Spain, in Baghdad, Kufa and Basra, in the main Islamic State, in Fustat, and Alexandria, in Africa, in Nishapur and Shiraj in Persia, in Bukhara and Samarqand in Southern Russia.

3
Imam Abu Hanifa

"Say: truth is come and falsehood is vanished."
(Qur'an 17:81)

Islam insists on the attainment of knowledge, to the extent that it has been made a pre-condition for all those who want to be included within the fold of Islam. Without proper knowledge of the Qur'an and the *Sunna* or without, at least, the rudiments of the main teachings of the Qur'an and *Sunna* a man cannot be a Muslim. A Muslim has to be sufficiently knowledgeable with regard to Qur'an and *Sunna* if he wants to follow Islam.

The Qur'an itself has laid the greatest emphasis on attaining knowledge. It says,

Are they equal, those who know and those who do not know? It is those who are endued with knowledge that receive admonition. (Qur'an 39:9)

And,

The blind and the seeing are not alike, nor are the darkness and the light. (Qur'an 35:19)

And,

Are the blind equal with those who see? Or the depths of darkness equal with light. (Qur'an 13:16)

The Prophet said,

> The ink of a scholar is holier than the blood of a martyr.
>
> To seek knowledge is obligatory on every Muslim.
>
> Seek knowledge even unto China.
>
> Those who go out in search of knowledge are fighting in the way of Allah until they return.
>
> Seek knowledge from the cradle to the grave.

It is because of this unique emphasis on knowledge given by the Qur'an and *Sunna* that we have seen the emergence of great Islamic scholars and intellectuals in every age of Islam. And it was more so in the great early days of Islam when it was the practice to learn the Qur'an by heart and to hold elaborate deliberations and discussions on the learning of *hadiths*. There were thousands of Qur'an readers, i.e. Qur'an memorisers, in the early Umayyad and Abbasid periods.

It is said that in the Battle of Yamama four thousand Qur'an memorisers were killed and this led to 'Umar ibn al-Khattab urging the Khalif, Abu Bakr, to indicate that the Qur'an should be written down as a book in the form we find it today. And it was because of his urging that Abu Bakr set up a committee to record the Qur'an with Zayd ibn Thabit as its chief.

Memorising and teaching the Qur'an were made a condition of dower (*mahr*) for those bridegrooms who were unable to pay anything else. If they undertook to teach the Qur'an and help their brides to learn it by heart they were exempted from paying the *mahr*.

Similarly attendance of *hadith* teaching circles and *hadith* discussions in mosques, assemblies and private houses were a part of the embellishment of Muslim aristocracy. Men and women vied with each other in memorising as many *hadiths* as possible. It is said that during the time of Imam Abu Hanifa or Imam Malik or Imam ash-Shafi'i or Imam Ahmad ibn Hanbal there were scholars who used to commit to memory fifty thousand to one hundred thousand *hadiths* each. Imam ash-Shafi'i, it is said, learned more than a hundred thousand hadiths by heart, and so did Imam Malik. There were several thousand scholars during this period who memorised this number of *hadiths*. The famous *Muwatta'* of Imam Malik was learnt by heart by Imam ash-Shafi'i so that on occasions he used to read out the whole *Muwatta'* by heart at a single sitting.

And the added splendour of this noble occupation was such that each of them knew the whole Qur'an by heart as well. Imam Abu Hanifa, Imam Malik, Imam ash-Shafi'i and Imam ibn Hanbal were each first a *hafiz* of the Qur'an and then a *hafiz* of *hadith*. And they were not just a *huffaz* or memorisers. They were great commentators on the Qur'an, they were great authors, they were great scholars and above all they were great leaders of Islamic thoughts and ideas. Each of them has left a line of *Shari'a* thinking which the Muslim *Ummah* all over the world are now following in the wake of their studies and pursuits. Today the Muslim *Ummah* are proud of the legacy of these great Imams who pioneered the cause of Qur'anic knowledge and the knowledge of *hadith*.

Imam Abu Hanifa was a most enlightened and scholarly person. He used to depend on a rational approach to problems. He was the pioneer of *qiyas* as an important factor in establishing Islamic law and on the *ijma'* of the *Ummah* as a source of Islamic law.

While he was staunchly supporting this cause there were several fundamentalist forces that were opposing him tooth and nail. But ultimately his "group of rational thinkers" won the day and he was acclaimed the leader or the forerunner of this thinking. It is because of his contributions to Hanafi thinking that the Muslim *Ummah* were able to combine the true light of the guidance of the revealed *Shari'a* with true and correct reasoning. He is said to have written several thousand original books and treatises on different aspects of Islam, many of which are still available in the libraries of the Muslim world.

Many of his disciples were prominent in the history of Islam. Three of his disciples, Muhammad, Abu Yusuf and Ja'far, along with thirty-seven other famous scholars formed a committee of jurists who were entrusted with the work of writing down the Book of Islamic Jurisprudence. The committee after thirty years of continuous studies and researches produced an Encyclopaedia which now no longer exists, probably burnt during the Hülügü holocaust of Baghdad in 1258. A glimpse of this holocaust by a European historian is reproduced below for the enlightenment of our readers:

> The city was systematically looted, destroyed and burnt. Eight hundred thousand persons are said to have been killed. The Khalif Mustasim was sewn up in a sack and trampled to death under the feet of Mongol horses.
>
> For five hundred years, Baghdad had been a city of palaces, mosques, libraries and colleges. Its universities and hospitals were the most up-to-

date in the world. Nothing now remained but heaps of rubble and a stench of decaying human flesh. (Sir John Bagot Glubb)

4
Imam Abu Hanifa
Part II

This section was written as a reply to a letter by Mr. Md. Tajiruddin Paramanik of Karatia College, published in the Bangladesh Observer on 18 February 1986, in response to my article published in the same publication on 31 January 1986 under the heading *Muslims' Contributions to Knowledge and Science.*

The learned commentator has done me an invaluable service by pointing his critical pen towards me and by quoting some Western sources. His letter betrays his blind dependence on Western sources. This happens all too often in connection with Islamic history and Islamic heritage. Does the learned commentator not know that Imam Abu Hanifa was born in 80 AH, just seventy years after the demise of the Prophet Muhammad and thus that he met many of the *Tabi'un*, those who met, lived and mixed with the *Sahaba* of the Prophet.

So all those Muslims who lived before the time of Imam Abu Hanifa were directly or indirectly associated with the *Sahaba* or *Tabi'un*, and as such there was no need for any guidance. Moreover, the energy generated by the Prophet and his *Sahaba* and their *Tabi'un* was sufficiently strong to hold together the Muslim *Ummah* for at least one hundred years.

Then came the need for a clear direction when the Muslim *Ummah* was divided into the followers of the Umayyads and the Abbasids, and further into the Kharijites and the Sunnis, and further into the oppressors and the oppressed. The extent to which the situation had deteriorated can be imagined from the following extract from a book by Syed Manazir Ahsan Gilani published by the Islamic Foundation, Dhaka:

> Imam Abu Hanifa was born at a point of the Umayyad Khilafat when the Muslim Ummah was shivering under the steam-rollering oppression of Umayyad misrule and injustice... For a long period the Prophet's mosque was not visited by any *Musalli* except by the only surviving *Sahabi*, Sa'id ibn al-Musayyab.
>
> Imam Abu Hanifa then saw the period of the dissolution of the Umayyad dynasty and the murder of its last Khalif Marwan II at the hands of the first Abbasid Khalif, as-Saffah. He also saw the rise of the second Abbasid Khalif, Abu Ja'far Al-Mansur, in whose hands he died very cruelly and tragically.

The learned commentator by quoting Western and some Eastern sources has asserted that Imam Abu Hanifa did not write a single book. Here are just some of his authentic books:

(1) *Kitab as-Salah* (2) *Kitab al-Manasik* (3) *Kitab ar-Rahan* (4) *Kitab ash-Shurut* (5) *Kitab al-Fara'id* (6) *Kitab al-'alim wa'l-muta'allim* (7) *Kitab al-'Asrar* (8) *Kitab ar-Risala* (9) *Kitab al-Irja'* (10) *Kitab al-Wasiya* (11) *Kitab Radd 'ala'l-awzah* (12) *Kitab ar-Ra'y* (13) *Kitab Ikhtilaf as-Sahaba* (14) *Ikhtilaf Abi Hanifa wa Abu Layla* (15) *Kitab al-Jami'* (16) *Kitab as-Siyar* (17) *Kitab al-Awsat* (18) *Kitab Fiqh al-Akbar* (19) *Kitab Fiqh al-Absat* (20) *Kitab ar-Radd 'ala'l-Qadiriyya* (21) *Risala* to 'Uthman al-Batti (22) Added to this should be literally hundreds of letters and pamphlets.

Allama Mahmud Hasan Khan Tunki of Hyderabad

University, Deccan, in his *Mu'jam al-Musanniffin* in sixty volumes (only thirteen volumes published so far) has referred extensively to Imam Abu Hanifa's book *Kitab ar-Radd 'ala-Awzah*.

Ibn Abi'l-Awam discussed and wrote many books on Imam Abu Hanifa's book *Kitab ar-Ra'y*. Abu Asim Al-'Amiri and Maswood ibn Abi Shu'ba referred profusely to Imam Abu Hanifa's book *Kitab Ikhtilaf as-Sahaba*. 'Abbas ibn al-Mus'ab in his *Tarikh al-Maru'* discussed and drew immensely from Imam Abu Hanifa's book *Kitab al-Jami'*.

Shaykh az-Zahid al-Kawsari in his book *Bulugh al-Amani* (pp. 18-19) referred to another twenty-one authentic books by Imam Abu Hanifa named *Masanid* on *Hadith* in his book *Tanib* while discussing the *Radd 'ala Khatib al-Baghdadi* on page 156.

As-Suyuti in his book *Tabriz as-Sahifa fi Manaqib Imam Abu Hanifa* has observed that Imam Malik wrote his famous *Muwatta'* after the pattern of Abu Hanifa's *Kitab al-Asrar*. Imam Muwaffaq Makki in his book *Manaqib Imam al-A'zam* has written that Imam Abu Hanifa wrote his famous *Kitab al-Asrar* after selecting 40,000 *hadiths* which were only a few out of his seventeen volumes filled with *ahadith* of the Prophet Muhammad.

Our learned commentator possibly does not know that Imam Abu Hanifa was the first revolutionary writer of Islam, the founder of Islamic law and jurisprudence and was poisoned/caned to death while in jail by Khalif al-Mansur for his unyielding role in refusing to issue *fatwas* favouring the Khalif. He preferred death to yielding to royal pressure to agree to their offer or rather their bribe of the post of the Chief Justice of the empire. It was he who separated justice and law from the administration and it was he who became the first martyr to the cause of justice and equity.

The great historian and scientist al-Khawrizmi wrote that Imam Abu Hanifa's council of forty jurists (who worked for thirty years),

> "...produced eighty-three thousand decisions/conclusions/*mas'alas* out of which thirty-eight thousand related to basic Islamic laws and the other forty-five thousand dealt with business and commercial rules and regulations." (*Imam Abu Hanifa*, p. 164, by Sayyid Manazir Ahsan Gilani)

Each of these eighty-three thousand decisions, *mas'alas*, is a treatise on Islamic law on the authority of Imam Abu Hanifa and as such he is the author of all these eighty-three thousand *mas'alas*. That is why the Muslim *Ummah* proudly call him the Imam al-A'dham.

5
Imam Ja'far as-Sadiq and Jabir ibn al-Hayyan

Did you think that We had created you in jest, and that you would not be brought back to us to render account? (Qur'an 23:115)

The contributions made by the early Muslim scholars to the field of knowledge and science were so enormous and far-reaching that the whole world drank deep from these fountains of knowledge. And the scholars and the seekers of knowledge from all countries of the world converged on the cities of Baghdad, Damascus, Kufa, Toledo, Granada, Cordoba, Tus, Bukhara, Shiraz, etc. These scholars received all kinds of state patronage from the Muslim kings and they were freely enrolled as teachers and students irrespective of their caste or creed in the different Islamic institutions and universities of these cities. They could be found receiving education and imparting education by consulting and exchanging books, dictionaries, treatises, all of which were abundantly available in all these cities. And these books were made available free of cost to all those seekers of knowledge irrespective of their caste or creed or nationality.

These seekers of knowledge had one common aim and that was to enrich their inquisitive minds with the knowledge available in the institutions and in the libraries of these cities. The Christians, the Jews, the Hindus and the Muslims from Europe, from Asia, from Samarqand, from Bukhara, from Iran and from all countries of the Middle East were concentrating on Baghdad and Kufa in the East, and on Toledo and

Cordoba in the West, to drink deep from the fountains of knowledge. These cities were fountains of learning with thousands of enlightened scholars of Islam enlisted as teachers, all getting salaries and other benefits from the state. None of the students was charged tuition fees nor was any required to pay for his board and lodging. All were given free education and free food and free lodging.

That these seekers of knowledge were enjoying a free and fair and frank atmosphere is borne out by the following fact of history. A Christian missionary who was at the court of the Khalif Al-Ma'mun became a great favourite of the Khalif because of his vast learning and devoted services. The Khalif asked him at one stage why he did not accept Islam when he knew Islam so thoroughly? The missionary remained silent and gradually slipped away from the Khalif's court. The next year he arrived again and informed the Khalif of his desire to became Muslim. The Khalif asked the reasons of his delayed decision and he replied that after he had left the court the previous year, he had occupied himself by writing down copies of the Bible and the Qur'an and in selling them in the market. While making copies he made alterations and deliberate mistakes to test the knowledge and faith of the buyers. But he found out that all the copies of the Bible were sold out, but none of the copies of the Qur'an were sold; and if one or two copies were sold they were returned later with the discrepancies pointed out. This whole episode confirmed his belief that the Qur'an was the revealed Book and the followers of the Qur'an were genuinely faithful.

Imam Ja'far as-Sadiq (700 - 765AD) was a great scholar, an *'allama'*, a physician, a philosopher, and a spiritual leader. He had extensive knowledge of the

Qur'an, *Hadith, Fiqh, Tafsir* and *Mantiq,* or logic. But he attained a surpassing knowledge in astronomy and in the science of medicine. It is said that he wrote more than five hundred books on health care which were compiled and annotated by another great scholar and scientist of Islam, Jabir ibn al-Hayyan.

This Jabir ibn al-Hayyan is considered the father of chemistry and he wrote more than two thousand books and treatises on different aspects of science and chemistry. The scientists of the modern world known him as "Geber", the greatest Arab chemist and the forerunner of all those who have studied in the field of chemistry. He wrote innumerable books on medicine and related subjects such as health care, on minerals, metals, stones, geology, the science of geometry, etc. His book *al-Jawhar* is an original book on medical science which is still referred to by Western scientists as an original attempt at medical science. His last testament that he left for posterity is as follows:

> My wealth and property will be taken away by my children and other relations. But the wealth of my contributions to knowledge and science will shine as a crown at the door-step of knowledge.

6
Nizamiyya Madrasa of Baghdad

O mankind! Fear your Lord, for the convulsion of the Hour of Judgement will be a terrible thing. (Qur'an 22:1)

Cruel and fanatical, the Leonese rarely gave quarter; when they captured a town they usually put all the inhabitants to the sword. Tolerance such as that accorded by the Muslims to the Christians could not be expected of them. (*The Moslems in Spain*, R. Dozy)

It has been the practice of many Western historians to decry the part played by the Arabs in the empire which they created and to point out that the artists, the philosophers, the scientists were individually of Persian, Armenian, Greek or Spanish origin. It is true, of course, that the original Arabs of Arabia who gave the first and decisive impulse to imperial conquest were far too few in number to populate an empire. (*The Empire of the Arabs*, Glubb)

The Arab mentality seemed peculiarly adapted to the study of mathematics and, in this field, they did much original work. They seemed to have a great gift of lucidity, and were remarkably clear organisers and classifiers - qualities essential to mathematics. Mansoor had collected many learned men at his court, particularly engineers and astronomers. He had also taken great interest in astrology, and frequently consulted astrologers about the future. In the khalifate of Ma'mun, an astronomical observatory was established. An Arabic work, *The Compendium of Astronomy by Al-Ferghani*, was in use in Europe until the sixteenth century. (*The Empire of the Arabs*, Glubb)

The Arabs made Algebra an exact science - the name itself is Arabic - *al-jubr*. They also laid the foundations of analytical geometry. They were indisputably the founders of plans and spherical trigonometry which, properly speaking, did not exist among the Greeks.

Some controversy has taken place on the question of who discovered zero, and it would now appear probable that the Arabs obtained the idea from China or India. The use of zero enables us to reckon in tens and hundreds and it thus forms the very basis of modern arithmetic. Even if the Arabs did not invent it, they were using it two hundred and fifty years before it reached Western Europe.

The fact that all this learning was widely diffused among the people is emphasized by the fact that there were at this time no less than one hundred bookshops in the Baghdad suburb of Karkh alone. There was also a library attached to every mosque. In 820 AD, Mamoon founded a central library in Baghdad which he called 'The House of Wisdom'. In Cordoba, at about the same time, there were no less than seventy libraries." (*The Empire of the Arabs*, Glubb)

> The greatest fact of all the facts is that 'people never learn from history,' but history goes on repeating itself and leaving its lessons for people. A rugged, strife-torn and mountaineering people who were known for their chaotic habits and pursuits were suddenly turned into an indomitable Arab force, which achieved a series of splendid victories unparalleled in the history of nations, for in the short space of ninety years that mighty range of Saracenic conquest embraced a wider extent of territory than Rome had mastered in the course of eight hundred. (*History of the Saracens*, Ockley)

How was it possible? It was possible because this indomitable force got the fire of inspiration from a Book called Al-Qur'an and from a man called Muhammad. This Book and this man were as inseparable as the head from the body and their collective influence on their followers was so great that mankind has yet to find a second instance like it. And the result was that as long as these followers remained faithful to this Book and to its bringer, they went on conquering country after country, winning war after war, overcoming nation after nation. No force in this world could stand in their way, and every possible opposition had to give in to make way for their onward march. They were invincible.

They were invincible because they were following the Truth. And when you are following the Truth you do not concern yourself with winning or losing. A follower of Truth is mad for the Truth itself; he is anxious to establish the Truth. And in establishing the Truth all obstacles and handicaps will be trampled underfoot and all finer qualities will be achieved and mastered.

The followers of the Qur'an in those days had as their goal the mastering of these finer qualities. They were the greatest warriors, they were the greatest heroes, they were the greatest benefactors, they were the greatest bestowers, they were the greatest patrons of science and education and they were the humblest of human beings. Once during the khalifate of 'Umar ibn 'Abdu'l-'Aziz, his slave, while performing the duty of fanning him, suddenly fell asleep; when the khalif saw this he took up the fan and started fanning the slave, until he (the slave) woke up.

The Nizamiyya Madrasa of Baghdad during the Abbasid period was famous for its scholars, scientists, educationists, jurists and philosophers. Men of learning from all over the world including Greece, Spain, France, Italy, India, even of China, pursued them in this great citadel of education. It is said between ten and twenty thousand students were pursuing higher studies at this institution. More than five thousand scholars of exceptional ability from different corners of the world were engaged in imparting lessons to these seekers of knowledge. These scholars were not necessarily Muslims. Many of them were Christians, Jews or others. Imam al-Ghazzali for a long time was the principal of this Madrasa and it was he who used to engage all these scholars and students in debates and discussions to seek the Truth.

All the Greek, Chinese and other literature available in those days in the world was brought to Baghdad and translated, edited, printed, and reprinted at government cost and then freely distributed among the public. So great was the patronage of this learning by the kings and princes in Baghdad that people of all religions, of all castes and colours from all over Europe, Asia and Africa, used to converge on the courts of the Khalifs. The greatest of the patrons of learning was Khalif Ma'mun.

7
Khalif al-Ma'mun

Say: O my Lord, let my entry be by the Gate of Truth and Honour; and likewise my exit be by the Gate of Truth and Honour (Qur'an 17:80)

Thus knowledge and science were fostered by the patronage of Muslim Khalifs and princes. They not only patronised the pursuit of science and other general knowledge but were themselves great students of science. They took an active interest in studying the science and they invited scholars from all over the world to visit their courts with new inventions, discoveries, research reports and dissertations.

> By Mamoon's time medical schools were extremely active in Baghdad. The first free public hospital was opened in Baghdad during the Caliphate of Haroon-ar-Rashid. As the system developed, physicians and surgeons were appointed who gave lectures to medical students and issued diplomas to those who were considered qualified to practise. The first hospital in Egypt was opened in 872 AD and thereafter public hospitals sprang up all over the empire from Spain and the Maghrib to Persia. (Glubb)

All this sophisticated knowledge and science could not be pursued without the active interest of the Khalifs. Why were the Khalifs so intensely interested in the pursuit of knowledge? They were so because they knew that without knowledge they would not able to fulfil their mission on this earth. They knew that knowledge was power; they also knew that public service was service of Islam; they also knew that without people's welfare their rule and mission would be a failure; they knew that they were carrying out the torch of light to all humanity. This was at a time when most of humanity was living in very primitive conditions in most European countries, including England and France.

Knowledge in Islam is so important that the Prophet of Islam asserted that to seek knowledge was holier than fighting on the battlefield in the way of Allah and commanding people to seek knowledge even unto China and saying that the pursuit of knowledge was an obligation for every Muslim, man and woman.

But the question arises of which knowledge should be acquired. There are millions of knowledgeable people throughout the world, but they are unable to recognise their Lord. They have only recognised the "glitter" of this world. To them life means the fulfilment of their carnal desires. Anything beyond carnal desires, beyond matter, is not understandable to them. They see nothing but matter and thus they are materialists.

> Knowledge by itself does not give any excellence. It is the use to which it is put that determines its quality. For extolling moral values, it is like a faithful friend; for serving baser objectives of life, it is like a serpent.
> *Jalaludin Rumi*

But Islam says life is not only matter. It is matter and spirit. Matter decays, spirit remains. Matter is destroyable, spirit is undecaying and permanent. So a man must not run after matter, even though it might be attractive and glittering, but should concentrate on his spirit which is going to stay with him permanently and eternally.

This spiritual knowledge is the knowledge which one should aspire to attain. And if a person succeeds in attaining knowledge of the spirit, then he succeeds in knowing the secrets of the universe, the metaphysics of Nature. And when he knows the secrets of Nature he knows his Lord. Then he will not need to run after this world. The world will run after him. But he will not take notice of this ensnaring world.

Without true knowledge a man remains no better than an animal. True knowledge comes from Allah. And that is why the Prophet said,

> The best of you is the one who has learnt the Qur'an and then taught it.

The best of men is he who has been gifted with true knowledge of the Qur'an and the *Sunna*. It is for this reason that the Prophet said,

> The knowledgeable persons (of Qur'an and *Sunna*) are the heirs of the Prophets.

When the early Muslims went on conquering country after country, they conquered the spirits of people and not the lands. What they wanted was to spread the Message, the Truth, and never out of vengeance or for the wealth of this world. They wanted to establish the rule of Allah on this earth, not man-made rule. Muhammad ibn Qasim's invasion of India originated from just such a spirit and aspiration to establish justice on this earth.

> When a country is populated by unbelievers it can remain as it is, but when it is populated by unjust people it cannot be permitted to remain as it is. 'Ali ibn Abi Talib.

The idea of the equality and brotherhood of all Muslims comes from true knowledge. When a man knows that the pride and arrogance of men of this world are nothing but the cause of ruination, he will surrender to his Lord. And the moment he surrenders he is a Muslim. And all great Muslims of this world have merely contributed to the central fact of knowledge that Allah is the Source of all knowledge and that if he wants to succeed in this world man has to drink deep from this source.

8
Muhammad ibn Musa al-Khwarizmi

We have explained things in various ways in the Qur'an in order that they may receive admonition, but it only increases their flight (from the Truth) (Qur'an 17:41)

Khalif Al-Ma'mun's period of rule (813 - 833) may be considered the 'golden age' of science and learning. He had always been devoted to books and to learned pursuits. His brilliant mind was interested in every form of intellectual activity. Not only poetry, but also philosophy, theology, astronomy, medicine and law, all occupied his time. (Sir John Glubb)

In Baghdad al-Ma'mun opened an institution which he called the "House of Wisdom" or "Daru'l Hikma," the principal object of which was the translation of foreign books. Abu'l-Faraj, the famous writer of *Kitab al-Aghani,* wrote that Khalif al-Ma'mun was deeply convinced that those who were given to reasoning and were followers of free conscience were the close servants of Allah and were very dear to their Lord. Al-Ma'mun also believed that "all intellectuals in learning were the torch-bearers and educators of men in this world." And that is why he invited the famed physicians, scientists, mathematicians, astrologers, historians, poets, lawyers, *muhaddiths* and *mufassirs* from all over the world and offered them all facilities and state patronage to encourage them to devote themselves to the pursuit of learning and original thinking. Al-Ma'mun succeeded, through their efforts, in translating most of the original works of Hebrew and Greek languages into Arabic.

> These intellectual giants not only translated several valuable works from those languages but they also wrote several original books. Most of them derived their inspiration from experimental knowledge and they did not believe in any assumptions. (Abu'l-Faraj)

> A certain Hunayn ibn Ishaq, a Christian, was in charge of translations from the Greek, Aristotle and Plato among the philosophers, Hippocrates and more especially Galen, among the physicians, were produced in Arabic. Many of these works, notably the seven volumes of Galen's *Anatomy* were subsequently to reach Western Europe in Arabic through Sicily and Spain. Hunayn himself was a physician and his ten treatises on the eye are the earliest known textbook of opthalamology." (Sir John Glubb)

> The most outstanding contribution of the Arabs to human knowledge was in the field of mathematics. They introduced the use of zero which, however, they may have learned from India or China. In contrast to the clumsy method of writing numbers employed by the Romans, the system used by the Arabs, reckoning in units, tens, hundreds and thousands, was to become the very basis of modern mathematics. Indeed we still refer to our method of writing figures as Arabic numerals. (Sir John Glubb)

The Arabs themselves invented algebra - itself an Arabic word - and also plane and spherical trigonometry. Al-Battani discovered trigonometrical ratios and invented sine and cosine, tangent and cotangent. Logarithms were discovered at the same time, the word being a corruption of the inventor's name, Al-Khwarizmi. An astronomical observatory was also established in the reign of Mamoon, whose astronomers measured the circumference of the earth with remarkable accuracy, six hundred years before Europe admitted that it was not flat. *The Compendium of Astronomy,* an Arabic work, was in use as a textbook in Europe until the sixteenth century. (Sir John Glubb)

The Arabs in the ninth century were experts in the art of gracious and refined living. Not only were members of the upper classes cultured, but slaves and concubines were expected to be equally accomplished. A good slave girl spent several years in special schools where she was taught refined manners and was expected to master the Arabic classics and to speak in an educated accent.

The evening parties in the salons of the wealthy were always of a high standard. After the day's work, people would change into clean clothes of bright and cheerful colours. The guests reclined on low couches spread with cushions and carpets, and scented with musk, myrtle and jasmine. Behind a screen an orchestra of slave girls sang and played on the violin, the lute or the guitar. The conversation was lively and intellectual, and would often include the recitation or improvisation of poetry" (Sir John Glubb)

The inventor of logarithms, Muhammad ibn Musa al-Khwarizmi, was born in 780 AD, and was brought up in the court of Al-Ma'mun by his father, Musa ibn Shakir, who was a high official in the palace. Al-Khwarizmi also took up a job in the Khalif's court and very shortly became a great favourite of the Khalif. He became an expert in Sanskrit language and translated into Arabic, under the orders of the Khalif the *Siddhantas* a Hindu astronomical book, and added several notes to it.

He was simultaneously a geographer, a mathematician and a philosopher. He translated Ptolemy's book on geography in 830 AD and drew up a large map of the world. He followed the latitudes described by Ptolemy but added the Muslim-conquered states in his book of geography. He also drew up under the orders of al-Ma'mun a large map of population and geography called *Surat al-Ard*. This map was accepted and followed as a model by western geographers while drawing the map of the world. In this map the earth was divided into seven zones in accordance with its climatic changes. By following his principles, the famous astronomers, al-Farghani (860 AD), Al-Battani (929 AD) and Ibn Yunus (1000 AD) developed the altitudes, latitudes and the galaxies which were later accepted as models in Europe.

Al-Khwarizmi, along with some of his colleagues, developed an astronomical counting table by which the distance and width of earth could be surveyed. This means he took the earth to be round. In 1226 AD,

Adelard of Bath translated his theory and the table into Latin and it later became thhe foundation of all astronomical studies and researches. Al-Khwarizmi's astronomical findings and theories were accepted in Greece, India and even in China.

But above all, al-Khwarizmi's original contribution was made in algebra of which the Muslims are the fathers. The name Algebra has been derived from his book *Hisab al-Jabr* and this fact has also been testified to by the great historian, Ibn Khaldun. It was from al-Khwarizmi that the Latin and European historians introduced the word, "algarism" and "algarithm" to express their derivations. The Latin word cipher meaning zero is from the Arabic word, *sifr*, which was also introduced by the Muslims. And al-Khwarizmi, the mathematician, was most probably the inventor of zero. The mathematicians of the world know this and acknowledge their debt to him.

9
Muhammad ibn Isma'il al-Bukhari

We bestowed wisdom on Luqman so that he showed gratitude to Allah, and anyone who is grateful, is so to the profit of his soul. (Qur'an 31:12)

The jurists of Islam were divided into two principal divisions, one was called the *Ahl ar-Ra'y*, or the people of intellect, and the other was the *Ahl al-Hadith*, or the people of *hadith*. Those jurists who used to put more emphasis on intellect and free exercise of conscience were from the first group, and those who adhered to *hadith* or *sunna*, putting less emphasis on free intellect, were of the second group. Imam Abu Hanifa belonged to the first group. They were also known respectively as "Iraqis" and "Hijazis".

Imam Abu 'Abdullah Muhammad ibn Isma'il al-Bukhari was born in 809 AD, and in his childhood he learnt the Qur'an by heart and then devoted himself to learning *hadith*. His memory was so sharp that if he heard a *hadith* once he could remember it with all its line of narrations throughout his life. He lived in Basra, Kufa and Madina for several years and dedicated himself to learning the *hadith* and their methods of collection and chains of transmission. He came in contact with Imam Ahmad ibn Hanbal and became his student. He also came in contact with and exchanged ideas with the famous *hadith* writers, Ibn Mubarak and Wuqay' and several other *muhaddiths* of his age. He learnt by heart all the books of *hadith* written by Ibn Mubarak and Wuqay'.

When he was twenty or twenty-five, he wrote two famous and influential books, *As-Sahaba wa at-Tabi'un* and

At-Tarikh al-Kabir. It is said that he wrote *Al-Tarikh* while sitting near the tomb of the Prophet on moonlit nights, and his hunger for history was so strong that he knew, at least, one incident about each historical personage.

Thereafter he went out in search of knowledge to Damascus, Egypt, Basra, Baghdad, Kufa, and came into contact with many of the Muslim scholars and *hadith* reciters of his age. Whenever he heard the name of a *hadith* reciter, he would rush to him without caring about the distance or difficulties of the road. Hunger for knowledge and *hadith* collection were his aim in life and he dedicated his life totally and wholeheartedly to the realisation of this aim. It is said that Imam al-Bukhari collected six hundred thousand *hadiths*, of which he learnt by heart two hundred thousand. Out of all these he accepted only one thousand *hadiths* as absolutely authentic in his *Al-Jami' as-Sahih*, and the rest he rejected.

He used to take very special care in selecting a *hadith*. Once he went a distance of some hundred miles to collect a *hadith* but, on arrival, he found the *hadith* reciter busy taming his horse by the false ploy of using a bag without fodder in it. He thought a man who could deceive his horse with such a false tactic would also be able to deceive his conscience by telling a lie. And so he turned back without hearing the *hadith* from him.

While he was busy collecting *hadith* during his forty yeasr of travels in Iran, Iraq, Egypt and the Hijaz, he met more than one thousand *hadith* reciters, sat with them, observed their ways of life and then heard their *hadith*. It is said that before writing a *hadith* he used to do ablution, say two *rak'ats* and then record the *hadith*.

His *Jami' as-Sahih* is considered to be the greatest of the hadith collections and is the pride of the entire

Muslim *Ummah*. Hundreds of books were later written on this book by hundreds of Muslim writers and scholars, of which *al-Kawakib ad-Darari* by Shamsu'd-din Muhammad Yusuf al-Kirmani (1348 AD), *Fath al-Bari* by Imam al-'Asqalani (1448 AD) and *'Umdat al-Qari'* by Imam Shaykh Badru'd-din al-'Ayni (1451 AD) are famous.

While Imam al-Bukhari was busy writing down the authentic *hadith* of the Prophet, there were a few more dedicated souls who also made their marks by recording the true *hadith* of the Prophet. Many of the *hadith* recorded by them were similar to each other's and so their authenticity became doubly sure. The five most famous *hadith* writers after Imam al-Bukhari were: Imam Abu'l-Husayn **Muslim** ibn al-Hajjaj an-Nishapuri (817-878 AD), Imam **Abu Dawud** (818—888), Imam Abu Musa **at-Tirmidhi** (823-893), Imam Muhammad **Ibn Majah** (823-886) and Imam 'Abdu'r-Rahman Ahmad **an-Nasa'i** (828-915). Imam al-Bukhari and these five *hadith* writers are called the *Sihha as-Sitta*, and they are well-known in Islamic history as the most authentic *hadith* compilers.

It is undoubtedly true that if these dedicated souls had not devoted their whole lives to collecting, analysing and selecting *hadith*, seperating the true from the false, we would not have been able to benefit from the golden blessing of the sayings of the Prophet. The true position of the *Sunna* after the Holy Qur'an would have disappeared had not these stalwarts of Islam dedicated their lives to its study. Humanity has learnt the true teachings of Islam through the services of these Imams and their scientific approach to the collection and selection of *hadith* has impressed even staunch and declared enemies of Islam.

10
At-Tabari

Such is Allah, your real Cherisher and Sustainer. Apart from Truth, what remains but error? How then are you turned away? (Qur'an 10:32)

Abu Ja'far Muhammad ibn Jarir at-Tabari was born in 838 AD of very poor parents in Tabaristan near the Caspian Sea. He had an unquenchable thirst for knowledge. In his childhood, he studied Persian language and literature, and Persia's history, and then left for Iraq to study Arabic language and literature, philosophy, logic and geology in Baghdad, at that time the centre of learning of the world.

While studying in Baghdad, he developed a great attraction for the Qur'an, *tafsir* and *hadith* literature. Later he went to Makka to specialise in the study of Qur'an and *hadith*, while associating himself with the great *'ulama'* of the time who were living in Makka. Then he visited Egypt, Syria, Iraq, Persia, etc. to widen his knowledge even further by seeking the company of Muslim scholars in those countries. During this long period he faced serious economic hardship and had to spend days and weeks at a time in a state of semi-starvation.

In later life he settled down in Baghdad and wrote his world-famous history and his Qur'an *tafsir*. He was a follower of Imam Abu Hanifa, and in his personal life, he was a very modest, religious and a self-respecting person. In his famous book of history he did not mention Imam Ahmad ibn Hanbal as an Imam and so the followers of the Hanbali school were furious with him and they tried to malign him as an enemy of Islam. They did not allow his public burial in Baghdad owing to their animosity to him on this account.

At-Tabari has retained an assured place in Islamic history as a great *mufassir* of the Qur'an. His *tafsir* of the Qur'an was written with such elucidation of erudite historical facts that the world, for the first time, got a new version of Qur'anic *tafsir*. In fact, he presented human history in the light of the teachings of the Qur'an and he awarded the world two magnificient gifts: human history in the light of the Qur'an and a Qur'anic *tafsir* which illuminated human history.

In those days, the Muslim writers dedicated their lives and everything they had to write books and histories of Islam. Their dedication and sacrifice knew no bounds. At-Tabari was the doyen of all these dedicated writers. The extent of his dedication and desire to pass on his knowledge can be guaged from the fact that he wrote a minimum of forty pages every day continuously for forty years.

The title of his famous history book is *Akhbar ar-Rusul wa'l-Muluk,* that is *The History of Prophets and Kings.* It is now available in fifteen volumes but the original book was written in one hundred and fifty volumes. It is said that when he found that his students were unwilling to study his one hundred and fifty volume *The History of Prophets and Kings,* he received a tremendous shock and he almost lost his senses. Then, as a compromise, he wrote down another fifteen volume history for his students which is now available in the libraries of the world. Incidentally, this is the first history of the world in Arabic.

He wrote down this famous history analysing the events of the world through the ages. He based his narration by taking the *Hijri* era as the turning point in human history. Starting from the pre-historic era, he narrated world events one after another in different ages and centuries until 302 AH(his age), that is, 915 AD. From each event he made an observation which he thought was fitting to that age. He wrote history to enable his readers to derive lessons from history.

At-Tabari also drew immensely from his immediate predecessors like Ibn Ishaq, Al-Kalbi, Waqidi, Ibn Sa'd, etc, who wrote in Persian. He also wrote down all the sagas and folk stories that he heard and noted during his long sojourns in several countries, including Makka and Madina. In his *History of Science* the historian Surton noted down that the great philosopher, Al-Farabi, the great mathematicians Abu Kamil and Ibrahim ibn Minan, the great geographer and lexicographer, Al-Mas'udi, and the great historian, at-Tabari, were all Muslims.

At-Tabari is famous among the Muslims for his great *tafsir* entitled *Jami' fi Tafsir al-Qur'an*, and it is available in thirty volumes in the libraries of the Muslim world. At-Tabari has used *hadiths* to the maximum extent in explaining the Qur'an. It is for this reason that his *tafsir* is so popular. This *tafsir* has given him an assured place as a great scholar and thinker of Islam.

11
Abu'l-Hasan al-Ash'ari

Do not invent simulitudes for Allah: for Allah knows and you know not. (Qur'an 16:74)

Abu'l-Hasan al-Ash'ari was born in 873 AD in Basra of parents who were themselves *'ulama'* . His forefather was the famous Abu Musa al-Ash'ari, the great Companion, who was one of the two mediators appointed after the Battle of Siffin by 'Ali ibn Abi Talib and Mu'awiya. The other mediator was 'Amr ibn al-'As.

His father Shaykh Isma'il was a renowned *'alim* of his time and he took special care to give the right type of education to his brilliant son in Qur'an, *hadith, fiqh, usul ad-din*, etc. from his early boyhood. The father took special care to educate the boy on the lines recommended by the *Shari'a* and he asked him not to get in touch with the Mu'tazilite group of scholars who were very active in those days and who were spreading their controversial ideas.

But Abu'l-Hasan frustrated all attempts of his father, went to Baghdad and became a disciple of the principal advocate of the Mu'tazilite group, Abu'l-Wahhab al-Jubba'i. Under his guidance he learnt philosophy, logic, and literature as well, and soon made his name as a good speaker and philosopher. But the Mu'tazilites had already, by that time, lost the power and patronage that they had previously enjoyed, and they were being hunted out by the enraged theologians and other Muslim scholars, who bore an inborn hatred towards the sect.

The Mu'tazilites used to interpret the Qur'an and *hadith* in a purely rationalistic way. They were known as "free thinkers" and they were influenced by the old Greek and other ancient philosophers from whom they borrowed freely when propounding their theories. In the name of the development of Islamic philosophy and Arabic literature, they borrowed so freely and indiscriminately from these alien sources that they lost touch with the Qur'an and *Sunna*. They started interpreting the Qur'an in a new way and held that the Qur'an was a "created" thing and that the *Miraj* took place in dream or by the imagination. In short, these Mu'tazilites by their resort to "free thinking" corrupted the roots of Islam from within and they convinced the luxury-loving Abbasid Khalifs, particularly Khalif al-Ma'mun, to accept their idea of the interpretation of the Qur'an.

It was through al-Ma'mun's patronage that the Mu'tazilites succeeded in establishing several institutes of learning, research cells, libraries, hospitals, astronomical observatories, higher centres of theological learning and discussion, but all leading to the Mu'tazila school of thought. In this way, these Mu'tazilites gradually captured all the key posts of the khalifate and they initiated a reign of terror by inflicting punishments on those *'ulama'* and scholars who were not in agreement with their school of thought. They used their high positions in the khalifate as an instrument to punish their opponents. So much so that they influenced Khalif al-Mu'tasim into inflicting a hundred stripe punishment on the famous scholar and Imam of a school of thought, Imam Ahmad ibn Hanbal (780-855 AD) for his opposition to their belief that the Qur'an was a "created" thing and subjected him to public humiliation.

It is reported that Imam Ahmad ibn Hanbal while

being whipped on a cart dragged through the streets of Baghdad shouted to the people to affirm that the Qur'an was indeed the uncreated word of Allah and that its every word and sentence was descended from Allah without any change or addition, and that on the Day of the Judgement people would see Allah with their eyes. It is also said that Imam Ahmad ibn Hanbal died of the whipping that he had received from these Mu'tazilites.

The people of Baghdad were so agitated at this whipping of a great scholar and Imam of Islam that they preceded in a great assembly to capture the inner courtyard of the palace. The orthodox Muslims led by the *'ulama'* were furious and the khalifate became alarmed at this agitation. At this time, the Khalif al-Mutawakkil became the ruler and he tried to soften the agitation by withdrawing the state patronage from the Mu'tazilites and by expelling the Mu'tazilites from the key positions in the state.

During this time, Abu'l-Hasan al-Ash'ari, sensing the decline of the Mu'tazilites, quietly left Baghdad and arrived in Basra, his birthplace. On a Friday prayer he stood in the Jami' Mosque of Basra and addressed the audience in the following words:

> Those who do not know me should know I am Abu'l-Hasan al-Ash'ari. I used to believe, before, that the Qur'an was a created thing, that we will not see Allah with our human eyes, and that we are the authors of our actions. Now I have turned to you, I have purified my beliefs from the cursed Mu'tazila school of thought. Now I believe that the Qur'an is descended direct from Allah. Its every word and spirit is from him. Everything of

> this world, good or bad, has been created by Him, and without His will nothing of this universe can exist. And we also believe that our Prophet will intercede for his *Umma*, and the *Mu'minin* will be saved from the Hellfire.

And so saying, al-Ash'ari removed all his upper garments and the *jubba* from his person, threw them under his feet, and said, "I tear off my old beliefs as I have torn off these clothes." Thereafter, he spent the remaining part of his life in countering the evil designs and wrong statements and wrong beliefs of the Mu'tazilites. Since he was earlier trained by the Mu'tazilites, he knew their weaknesses and sensitive issues and thus he started replying to their points one after another. He introduced the science of *al-Kalam*, that is scholastic theology which saved the Muslim nation from the cursed rationalism of the Mu'tazilites.

Soon he became widely acclaimed as a scholar throughout the Muslim world. The *'ulama'* all accepted him as their leader in their fight against the Mu'tazilites.

Abu'l-Hasan al-Ash'ari was a born genius. He wrote more than one hundred books on different subjects of Islam. Of these, his *Maqalat al-Islamiyya* is the greatest book on *'ilm al-Kalam*. In this book, he compared Greek philosophjy with Islamic philosophy and pointed out those things which are irrelevant to the requirements of Islam and made *'ilm al-Kal*am the basis of our philosophy. In this respect, he is the father of *'ilm al-Kalam* or Islamic theology, and Imam al-Ghazzali is its perfector.

The ideas and teachings of Abu'l-Hasan al-Ash'ari made their impact in the East. In its initial stage the Ash'ari school of thought was strongly opposed by the

Mu'tazilites, but gradually, with the strong support it received from the khalifate, particularly from men like Nizamu'l-Mulk and Imam al-Ghazzali, his doctrine became very popular all over the Muslim world. Al–Ash'ari and al-Ghazzali were criticised for their strong opposition to the study of science and philosophy for the sake of study only, without considering the need to study religion and the *Shari'a*. But it is they who saved the Muslim nation from the onslaught of the Mu'tazilites, who were taking the nation to secularism.

12
Muhammad Al-Farabi

The Truth is from your Lord, so be not at all in doubt. (Qur'an 2:147)

Abu Nasr Muhammad al-Farabi, also known as the *Mu'allim Thani* (Second Teacher) of the East, was born in 870 AD in Farab, a city now almost non-existent, in mid-Turkey. Once this city was the birthplace of several internationally famous intellectuals and philosophers of the Muslim world. The great Timur-i-leng (Tamerlane) breathed his last in this city.

Despite his prolonged stay in Iran, Iraq, Egypt, etc. he never changed his Turkish dress nor did he forsake his nickname, Farabi at-Turki, by which he was known. The Amir of Aleppo, Hamdani Sayfu'd-dawla, made him a member of his inner court when he found him an expert in eighty-nine languages, and a great scholar in Muslim *fiqh*, in philosophy, science, medicine, and even in poetry and music.

He was a man of short stature. He studied and spent his boyhood in Farab and then left for Bukhara where he accepted the post of *Qadi*. But his thirst for knowledge drove him on and made him give up the post of Qadi. He ended up in Baghdad, then the centre of learning of the world. Here he, at first, studied the Arabic language and then Greek. Then he studied Aristotle's philosophy and logic under the guidance of a famous philosopher Abu Bishr Matta ibn Yunus. It is said that he prepared seventy volumes of notebooks to jot down the sum and substance of philosophy. He then studied Arabic grammar under the famous grammarian and linguist Abu Bakr ibn Saraj.

Then he studied, under the guidance of several great scholars, arithmetic, physics, chemistry, medicine and astronomy. But despite his profound scholarship in several subjects, he excelled particularly in philosophy, and he remained immortal for his contribution to this subject.

He stayed in Baghdad for more than forty years (from 901-942AD) and during this long period he studied devotedly Aristotle's logic and philosophy and wrote a few original books on philosophy. During his stay in Baghdad six khalifs followed one after the other in quick succession and these changes in the khalifate and the chaos which resulted from them made life miserable for a man otherwise given to peace. Eventually he left Baghdad and stayed in Turkestan for some time. At this time, under the orders of 'Ali Sam'an, the local Amir, he wrote his famous book *at-Ta'lim ath-Thani*. It is to be noted that in the intellectual circles of the East, Aristotle is regarded as the father of philosophy and al-Farabi as the second father, or the *mu'allim thani*.

Al-Farabi then left for Syria and then for Egypt. But he soon returned to Syria and settled down in Aleppo. Meanwhile in 945 AD, Amir Sayfu'd-Dawla defeated and drove out the ruler of Syria and himself settled in Aleppo.

Al-Farabi, one day approached Amir Sayfu'd-dawla as an ordinary *musafir*, but the Amir having come to know of his great scholarship and contribution to learning, received him in his court with great honour. He at once gave him a very high position in the court, but the peace-loving and knowledge-thirsty al-Farabi asked for nothing but a four dirham state grant and a solitary room to enable him to devote himself to his studies and research, which was granted. He dedicated himself peacefully to his studies thereafter.

In 950 AD Amir Sayfu'd-dawla made an expedition to Damascus and took al-Farabi with him. But the eighty year old al-Farabi with his fragile body could not withstand the fatigues of this expedition and died soon after he reached Damascus. Amir Sayfu'd-dawla himself attended his *janaza* (funeral) and buried him in Damascus in the vicinity of the Bab as-Saghir near the grave of Amir Mu'awiya, the Companion of the Prophet and founder of the Umayyad dynasty. People from all walks of life even now visit his grave to pay their homage to this great drinker from the fountain of knowledge.

Al-Farabi wrote more than one hundred books in Arabic on philosophy, science, medicine, music, etc. but only a dozen or so books are still available in the libraries of the world. His books have been translated into different languages of both the East and West. His name is honourably remembered along with the greatest philosophers of the world. Among the Muslim philosophers his name is uppermost, followed by Ibn Sina and Ibn Rushd.

But he differed from Ibn Sina and Ibn Rushd in not involving himself in politics. Love for knowledge was the driving force of his life. His observations on Aristotle and Plato were remarkable. It is due to him that all other philosophers after him were able to recognise them. He is the first Muslim writer of encyclopaedic knowledge and the father of *mantiq* (Islamic logic). He is the man who gave correct and practical demonstration of syllogism with examples, and he is the one who introduced several modes of deductive method.

He transformeded Aristotle's Divine duality into one

God and he searched for Truth itself and succeeding in finding it through his high philosophy and mysticism. Based on his findings, a group of later philosophers known as the Ikhwan as-Safa and people like Ibn Sina, Nasru'd-din at-Tusi, as-Sulami, Imam al-Ghazzali, etc. perfected *tasawwuf*, or mysticism, in Islam. While analysing philosophy in the light of Islam he made extensive use of words like "revelation," *tasbih, risalat,* Heaven, Hell, *'Arsh, Kursi, Taqdir, taqlid,* etc. In this field, he is the father of Islamic philosophy vis-à-vis religion. In his opinion, prophecy is the greatest spiritual and ethical achievement and not the result of any birthright. And thus for him the position of philosophy is above a prophecy. For this he was bitterly criticised by the *'ulama'* class, particularly by the Shaykh al-Islam, Imam Ibn Taymiyya. Ibn Taymiyya issued a *fatwa* banning the study of philosophy.

Al-Farabi was the first to study society, and he is, in this respect the forerunner of Ibn Khaldun, another great historian and social scientist. Some people of the West regard Al-Farabi as the originator of Rousseau's *Social Contract*, and others make him the ancestor of the German philosopher, Immanuel Kant, with regard to his theory of Rational Morality.

In political thought, Al-Farabi is considered to be the father of the Arabs in political science. Al-Farabi studied extensively Plato's *Republic* and *The Laws*, and gave a new analytical explanation to political science. His formula is quite different from that of Plato. A thousand years ago it was he who gave the world the idea of ruling the world under one government. His five original books on political science are still available. They are: (1) *Siyasatu'l- Madaniyya* (2) *Arawal Ahlil* (3) *Madinatu'l-*

Fadila (4) *Jawami' as-Siyasa* and (5) *Ijtima' Madania*.

In short, he presented some rare original ideas to political science, which have still not been realised. He held that if someone embodying all the qualities is not available, then the state should be governed jointly by a group of rulers of particular qualities. This theory presaged the present system of having a council of ministers to run the administration.

His greatest book, *Ihsa al-'Ulum*, on philosophy had a tremendous influence on the philosophers of the world. Many philosophers have written criticisms of this book as well. His other important book, *Fusus al-Hikma*, is equally popular among the philosophers.

His profound scholarship in the field of medicine, although recognised by all, did not leave us any proof that, like his disciple, Ibn Sina, he practised medicine. His book on medicine, *Al-Madinat al-Fadila* is a popular book.

He also wrote books on music. His *Kitab al-Musiqa al-Kabir* is a well-known book on music. He is said to have invented a musical instrument whose name, according to several music experts, was *qanun*.

Al-Farabi died about a thousand years ago, but his following words of advice are remarkable:

> As the success of a tree lies in its fruits, so the success of morality lies in finding real peace, and the ultimate result of a constant moral life is perfect and genuine peace.

13
Al-Firdawsi

There has come to you from Allah a light and a perspicuous Book. (Qur'an 5:17)

Abu'l-Qasim al-Firdawsi was born in 920 in a village near Tus in the province of Khurasan. His father, Fakhru'd-din Ahmad was a village headman and a man of refined taste. He was also quite affluent and he gave his son a good primary education. In those days the state language of Khurasan was Arabic, although the language of the masses was Persian. Abu'l-Qasim learnt Arabic from his *'alim* father, but he specialised in Persian, his mother tongue.

According to the contemporary practice, he learnt *tafsir, hadith, fiqh,* history, philosophy, etc. but his mind was inclined to Iran's ancient stories and folklore. His genius was unusually sharp and his ready wit and intelligence were abundant. As a result he soon earned his name and fame as a scholar and a genius.

The ancient Sassanid kings were considered great heroes and their exploits and family trees were the stories loved by the common people. They used to have their glories and achievements recorded by men of learning and thus ancient Persia's history has been written. Abu'l-Qasim somehow got hold of a copy of this history of ancient Persia and he was very much attached to reading these stories. He started writing lyrics, poems and sagas about these ancient heroes which were highly praised and appreciated in intellectual circles.

Basing himself on this ancient history ofthe Persian Empire, he started writing his great epic, the *Shahnamè* and after twenty-five years of hard work and struggle he succeeded in presenting the *Shahnamè* in 999 AD to his patron Muhammad Ibn Bakr, ruler of the Khalijan province of Iran. The Persian intelligentsia were deeply appeciative of the epic and the general people enjoyed it immensely. Abu'l-Qasim was also elated by the success of his book.

But he did not stop there. He began to add new stories and new subjects to the epic. For ten years more he worked on this scheme with great dedication, and ultimately succeeded in making it one of the really momentous epics of the world. At that time Sultan Mahmud was the King of Ghazna and he was patronising and rewarding poets, philosophers, scientists, *'ulama'* of all kinds, and inviting them to come to embellish his court. Among his courtiers were the poet al-Ansari and the philosopher-scientist Al-Biruni. Abu'l-Qasim, having learnt of the great patronage of Sultan Mahmud, proceeded towards Ghazna and sought an audience with the Sultan. When the Sultan heard the poet's recitation and the presentation of the *Shahnamè*, he was enthralled with joy and surprise. He remarked to the poet in the following words, "O poet Firdawsi! You have turned my courtyard into a heaven!"

Thus Firdawsi became known to the whole world as the poet of Tus. He dedicated the revised and completed version of the *Shahnamè* to Sultan Mahmud of Ghazna. He became the favourite poet of the Sultan and started living in Ghazna as court poet. His name spread far and wide and his poems and lyrics were on everyone's tongues. But this situation did not last long. Several people both in and outside the court became jealous of the poet's fame. It is said that the Sultan's chief minister himself and the Sultan's confidant slave, Ayaz, were particularly jealous of him, and they started conspiring against him. How far this was true was not made clear by the historians, but it is true that Firdawsi had to leave Ghazna and seek refuge in Shiraz in one of his admirers' houses. Here in Shiraz he wrote his other famous epic, *Yusuf and Zulaykha*. Thereafter he left Shiraz and went back to Tus, his birthplace, where he lived quietly and died in 1020 or 1025 AD. Thousands of people every year visit his grave to pay their respects.

From his life it appears that he was exceptionally attached to Persia's ancient history. He was extremely partiotic, always sympathetic to other people's sorrows, very large-hearted, very sharp, unusually industrious, ideally patient and wonderfully witty. He was a natural poet. He spent his whole life in the service of poetry. His *Shahnamè* contains sixty thousand couplets and his *Yusuf and Zulaykha* contains five thousand couplets. Besides this he wrote hundreds of lyrics, songs and ghazals. He also wrote satirical poems.

But the *Shahnamè* is his masterpiece. It was his major work, a major contribution to Persian literature. In its lucid language, its thrilling narration, its character portrayal and its wonderful phraseology, there is no other epic in Persian which can match its excellence. For this the European scholars call him the Homer of the East. Indeed, in epic composition, there is no other book which can compare with it except, possibly, the *Ramayana* and *Mahabharata* of India.

For centuries people have enjoyedthe reading the *Shahnamè*, a book which has entertained the minds of all its readers and given relief to absorbed readers in their hours of thought, and diverted its readers when they

Continues on last page

14
Al-Biruni (973-1048 AD)

Thus We do make the wrongdoers turn to each other because of what they earn. (Qur'an 6:139)

Abu Rayhan Al-Biruni Muhammad ibn Ahmad was born on 4 September 973 AD, in Khwarizm, Uzbekistan, in what is now the U.S.S.R. The Persians claim him as a native of their own land, the Arabs claim him as a student of their culture and the Indians claim him as a great traveller of their country. He was known all over the world by his pen name, Al-Biruni.

He was brought to Ghazna along with his teacher, 'Abdu's-Samad Awwal, in the company of Sultan Mahmud's prisoners of war when in 1017 Sultan Mahmud defeated Sultan Mamuni of Khibar. 'Abdu's-Samad Awwal was hanged for his belief in Qarmatian doctrines and al-Biruni was also destined for the same fate but Sultan Mahmud's courtiers intervened and saved him on the grounds of his being a great astronomer. And so this famous astronomer was included in the court of the inner assembly of the Sultan's great intellectuals and scientists whose number was not less than four hundred. The poet Firdawsi was also included among them.

In his boyhood and youth, al-Biruni dedicated himself to all kinds of studies and he made his name in poetry, literature, history, geography, science, medicine, astronomy, etc. But he excelled in astronomy and he indeed attained a huge knowledge of this subject. At the age of 25, he was appointed by Sultan Mamuni as his astronomer. When he was brought to Ghazna, he became the chief advisor and royal astronomer of Sultan

Mahmud. According to some, he was to Sultan Mahmud as Aristotle was to Alexander the Great.

But al-Biruni had no liking for Sultan Mahmud's conquests and expeditions. He travelled to India with Sultan Mahmud following his conquests and stayed there for more than ten years, learning Sanskrit and Hindu astronomy. From his writings we know that he developed a great fondness for India as an aggrieved party for having been used as a target of Sultan Mahmud's attacks and conquests. In his opinion there is valour in conquering lands by fighting and bloodshed and there is credit in that. But there is no credit in destroying other people's culture and fine arts. That is why al-Biruni was never happy in his heart at Sultan Mahmud's conquests and expeditions in India. Despite the Sultan's clear love and dedication to Islam, al-Biruni's constant question to him was why repeatedly attack India. And, in fact, he never forgave Sultan Mahmud for his attacks on India and on its culture and fine arts. He also did not return to Ghazna during the Sultan's life-time.

The artist in Al-Biruni always had the upperhand over the conqueror in al-Biruni. In his old age he returned to Ghazna and became a favourite of Sultan Mahmud's son, Sultan Mas'ud. Mas'ud's son, Mawdud, also used to respect him and hold him in high esteem. Al-Biruni used to keep close contact with all intellectuals and scientists of time time. The famous philosopher, scientist and physician, Ibn Sina, was also with him once in the Sultan's court, and they became very close to each other, engaging in the discussion of many complex problems striving to find solutions for them.

We do not know anything about his family life. Historians are silent about it. He died on the 13th

December, 1048. He lived a very simple life. He used to remain absorbed in his books and writings. Two days in the year - *Nawruz* and *Miraj* Day - he used to observe as his holidays.

In the golden age of Muslim civilization, al-Biruni was one of the bright stars who gave their light to the world. The list of his many books, according to Ya'quti, his biographer, took up sixty pages but only twenty-seven have survived the ravages and vicissitudes of time. His greatest book, *al-Qanun al-Mas'udi wa'n-Najm*, on astronomy was a book that captured the attention of the entire world. This book is the greatest book on astronomy in the Arabic language. It is also an encyclopaedia inasmuch as it discusses geometry, trigonometry, calculus, etc. in great detail and seeks to solve many delicate and complicated arithmetical matters.

He discussed in this book how he was able to calculate the earth's circumference by surveying, while sitting on the peak of a mountain. The findings he arrived at are still held to be true and correct. It is said that when the *Qanun* was presented to Sultan Mas'ud, he was so moved that he sent an elephant with a load of silver coins on its back as a present to al-Biruni. But al-Biruni returned the entire load saying that he did not need any money and asked them to deposit it in the government treasury. A similar event happened in connection with Sultan Mahmud when he presented sixty thousand silver coins to the poet Firdawsi. However, acting in an opposite way to al-Biruni, Firdawsi was mortally hurt because he was expecting sixty thousand gold coins from the Sultan for his *Shahnamè*.

His other book on astronomy, *al-'Asr al-Baqia*, was published in Ghazna in 1019. In the preface to this book he said,

> To arrive at any truth, it is not enough to depend only on philosophical thoughts and on one's own experiments and findings. An understanding of the events of the world and the history of mankind and their correct analysis are a necessity if you desire to arrive at a truth. While searching for the secrets of nature one should proceed from the known to the unknown and from the close to the distant.

Modern scientists have accepted this precept of al-Biruni as a key in all their research work.

Al-Biruni was a great geographer and a traveller. He spent forty years of his life in travelling and meeting people. As a result he gained a varied experience of lands and people. While, on the one hand, he enriched his own knowledge and experience through these travels, on the other, he exchanged his ideas and thoughts on philosophy, astronomy and science with other astronomers and scientists. In India, he mixed freely with Hindu philosophers and astronomers, saw their deep superstition and narrow approach to several matters, and criticised them for their blindness and superstition. He was one of the first and Muslim thinkers and philosophers to study a non-Muslim civilization, their thinking and their art with respect, and then write about them with sympathy.

About India he wrote his book, *Tahqiq mal Hind*, and he discussed in detail the Hindu religion, their philosophy, their culture, their literature, their geography, their astronomy, their behaviour and their superstitions. That the Sind delta was once a part of the sea and gradually formed part of the land, was scientifically explained by him for the first time among the Indian scientists. It was he who admitted unhesitatingly that it was the Indian mathematicians who had invented zero and that the Arabs adopted it from them. He also translated a few Indian books into Arabic and a noted Arabic book on medicine into Sanskrit.

Al-Biruni is world-famous not only for his books on astronomy and on Hindu culture but also as a great scientist and mathematician. The earth's movement on its axis and the moon's movement around the earth, and latitude and longitude - all these topics he discussed in his research work. In physics he also made a significant contribution. His book *Al-Jamahir fi'l-Jawahir* describes in great length about physics and about metals and precious stones. In this book he showed his genius as a scientist and also as a poet and a rhymer as there are many humorous couplets in between the prose passages. He also wrote a few books on arithmetical geography and trigonometry. He wrote a few books on satire and fine arts. He wrote books on prose and a few on poetry.

In short, he was an all-round genius. He had vast command of the Arabic and Persian languages but he wrote all his major books in Arabic. The fact that he translated *Pathanjali* from Sanskrit into Arabic shows that he had learnt Sanskrit quite well. He knew Greek as well because he frequently quoted from the Greek poet, Homer, and the philosophers Aristotle and Plato.

Al-Biruni was a fine chess player. He also gave a few pieces of advice with regard to this game. He was Shi'a by faith and also a fatalist. In politics he was a conservative. In religion, philosophy and politics he was a votary of independent thinking. In his thinking, humanity and scholarship he was far above his many contemporaries and can justifiably be called their leader. The historian George Surton said that al-Biruni was one of the great scientists of all times and that his influence on Arab civilization could never be effaced.

15
Ibn Sina (980 - 1037 AD)

Verily Allah is with those who restrain themselves and those who do good. (Qur'an 16:128)

Abu 'Ali Husayn ibn Sina was a man of the eleventh century AD who became a man of all countries and all climes and who attained the highest place of honour and prestige all over the world by dint of his unequalled scholarship and mastery of knowledge. He is called *ash-Shaykh ar-Ra's* of knowledge. That is, he was the peak of knowledge. He is claimed by the Persians and the Turks as their man. Equally he is claimed by the Afghans and the Uzbekiss as the pride of their lands. But we must remember that these geniuses of knowledge belong to no land, they belong to the world. What they leave as contribution is their legacy for humanity in general.

In fact, this *Shaykh ar-Ra's* was born in Afsana in Bukhara in the state of Uzbekistan in modern USSR in the year 980. His father 'Abdullah and his mother Sitara were both of Persian descent, and that is why he wrote many poems and essays in Persian in his boyhood. But like his contemporaries, al-Biruni and others, he wrote all his books in Arabic.

His father 'Abdullah was an administrator in Bukhara and he arranged for the best education for his son. The son began to show his talent from the very beginning of his life. His memory and intelligence were unsurpassed. At the age of ten he learnt the Qur'an and attained mastery of the Arabic language. In his adulthood, he became a scholar of all learning and was given the title of *Hakim*, that is, the wise.

Ibn Khalliqan, the great biographer, tells us that at the age of sixteen Ibn Sina became the centre of attention of most of the famous doctors and *hakims* of his time. They used to visit him to discuss his new medical discoveries and his new formulae. At the age of 16 he cured the Samanid Sultan, Nuh ibn Mansur, of a serious ailment, and then he was appointed as the Sultan's royal physician. The Sultan also permitted him to use his famous library and thus enabled him to drink deeply of the rare books that were available there. At the age of 21, he took up the task of writing his lasting and immemorial books.

Ibn Sina's father was a Muslim of the Isma'ili sect. His house was the centre of activity of many great scholars and *'ulama'* of Islam who used to come to his house in crowds to discuss delicate points of philosophy and Islam. From these learned discussions, Ibn Sina benefited immensely and was able to grasp a wide knowledge of Islam. In this house he learnt Islamic philosophy, science and politics, which he later expanded with his wide-ranging studies.

Ibn Sina was a philosopher and scientist. But he was also a great administrator and he used to take an active part in the administration and politics of his state which he served as a minister under a succession of Sultans. He had to flee and remain in hiding in Bukhara, Hamadan and Isfahan for having declined a favour of Sultan Mahmud of Ghazna.

He was one of those who took this world as a field of their fullest activities to execute all their plans and dreams and to enjoy their fruits. He was of the belief that one should enjoy this world to the full and search out the secrets of nature to the fullest possible extent. On the one hand, he was an unrivalled philosopher, a great scientist and a remarkable statesman, and on the other, he was a frolicking entertainer given to the enjoyment of the pleasures and luxuries of this world. It is this lack of control and his wayward life that cut short the genius in him and he died rather a premature death at 57 in the year 1037 AD.

Ibn Sina was a prodigious worker. The whole day he remained extremely busy in settling the affairs of state, and in the night he was wrote his incomparable books which became masterpieces of the medical and philosophical worlds. In the famous book *Tarikh al-Hukama'* of al-Qifti there is a detailed description of Ibn Sina's 21 major books and 24 smaller works on the subjects of medicine, philosophy and science. Besides this, he also wrote about one hundred more booklets on different subjects like geometry, arithmetic, language, music, *'ilm a-kalam*, etc. Of them, his greatest books are *Kitab ash-Shifa'* in 18 volumes, *an-Najah* in ten volumes, *al-Hikma* in ten volumes (on philosophy) and *Qanun at-Tibb*. These four books were his greatest contributions to mankind. While his *ash-Shifa'* has made him one of the greatest physicians of this world, his *al-Hikma* has made him one of the greatest philosophers of the world. Many centuries have passed by, but his books *ash-Shifa'* and *al-Hikma* have remained there as a witness to his greatness.

Ibn Sina by his deep insight, by his wide intellect and by his liberal ideas on philosophy, particularly on Greek philosophy, have captured the minds of the intelligentsia of the whole world, particularly his mastery of Aristotle's views and thought. He gave a sound direction to the channels of Greek philosophical ideas and thought, and like al-Kindi, he rather improved them and perfected them in order to present them to the ever-enquiring intellectual world. In the words of Hitti, he was successful in adjusting and making a balance between the philosophical ideas of Islam and Greek ideas. In short, Ibn Sina served as a bridge between Aristotle and Islam, and he turned out to be a great supporter of Greek philosophy.

He believed that Allah's greatest blessing to humanity was faith and the power of reasoning. According to him man's greatest piety consisted in the development of his faculty of understanding and his intelligence. In short, he relied more on rationality than on blind faith and belief. But Islam urges a man to have blind faith in Allah and to have unquestioned belief in the hereafter. And here Ibn Sina came to a direct clash with Islam, particularly with the orthodox section of Muslim scholars. They branded him an atheist. Ibn Sina also did not believe in the physical rebirth of the dead after their death. He also did not believe in physical enjoyment or punishment in heaven or hell. But he was an ardent believer in Allah and His Prophet, and he also used to perform the requirements of Islam.

In the field of medicine, particularly in Hakimi medicine, Ibn Sina was the greatest among the Muslim scholars. For many centuries Ibn Sina was a great name in Europe. For at least six centuries he was the undisputed leader of medical theorists and druggists. His famous book *al-Qanun fi't-Tibb* was the chief medical reference work. All kinds of rare medical information and references were available in this book. It was a great condensation of Unani and Hakimi medicines. In it all kinds of treatment and symptoms of diseases are elaborately described. Over seven hundred prescriptions and their uses and benefits were mentioned in the pharmacopoeia of this book.

It was first translated into Latin in the twelfth century by the famous physician Gerard. This translation was accepted with great welcome throughout Europe. It was included in the textbooks of all medical institutions all over Europe. From the 12th century to the 17th century, Ibn Sina was the great teacher of all medical science, and his *Qanun* was the principal textbook in medical science throughout Europe.

Ibn Sina made continual researches into discovering a medical cure from gold and silver. It may not be out of place to imagine that it was possibly Ibn Sina who may have introduced the present system of enveloping the tablets of medicine with a sheet of gold and silver. He also developed a cure for the cataracts of eyes.

Besides his *Qanun,* his great book, he also wrote fifteenother books on medicine which are also consulted by doctors and physicians. This great father of medicine and great leader of philosophy is lying buried in Hamadan where many visitors from the West and East go to pay their homage. The *Hakims* of the countries from Morocco to India and Indonesia even now give prescriptions for diseases in accordance with the practices followed by Ibn Sina.

16
Imam al-Ghazzali (1058-1111 AD)

And admonish your nearest kin. (Qur'an 26:214)

In the eleventh century, the Muslim world was in turmoil. On the one hand, Christian Europe has set out to destroy the Muslim world through the Crusades, and on the other hand, to challenge Muslim rule in Spain. Still a proliferation of sects and *tariqas* and ideologies; and above all, the evil influence of Greek and Indian philosophy on the Muslim educated class - all these forces were driving the Muslims away from their religion. At this critical juncture Imam al-Ghazzali appeared like a bright star on the scene and directed his sharp pen against these evil forces. In human history very few men have been able to make their mark as he did on human thought, on human endeavour and on man's search for knowledge.

There are geniuses in this world who preach things but do not practise them. But Imam al-Ghazzali was one of those who preached, wrote and spread only those things which he practised. This immortal genius and thinker was born in 1058 in Tus in the province of Khurasan. His real name was Abu Hamid ibn Muhammad an-Nishapuri. "Ghazzali" was a title taken probably from his birthplace, Ghazala, or from his father's trade, *Ghazzal*, meaning wool merchant. His father was a very religious Sufi who used to find special pleasure in associating with Sufis and dervishes.

He started his career with a great Sufi who gave him lessons in the Qur'an, *Hadith* and Sufism. He then studied the *Shari'a* for some time with Shaykh Ahmad at-Tusi and then he went to Jurjan to become a disciple of Imam Abu Nasr of Jurjan. While he was returning from Jurjan to Tus, he was attacked by bandits and robbed of all his belongings, including his books and manuscripts. Then he went to the leader of the bandits and requested him to return his books and manuscripts in return for keeping everything else. At this the bandit leader remarked with laughter that if they had looted his knowledge, then there was no need for such knowledge. If his knowledge was confined to books, could he really be called a man of knowledge? This taunting remark went deep into his heart and thereafter he started memorising everything that he had learnt.

Then for some time he devoted himself to studying Sufism and in 1078 he was admitted into the famous Nizamiyya Madrasa of Nishapur and became a disciple of the principal of the Madrasa, Shaykh Abu'l-Ma'ali, the Imam of the Haramayn. Under his leadership, he learnt religion, philosophy, jurisprudence and natural law. Everyone in the Nizamiyya Madrasa was struck by his profound learning and unusual genius. The Imam al-Haramayn himself had said to him out of jealousy, "You have outdone me while I am alive! You could have at least waited until I died!"

At this time he became more prone to criticising faith than having faith. He used to declare that those who did not judge and discern could not find the truth - they would remain in the dark. He used to believe, at this time, that the scholars should only reach a conclusion through research and discerning the truth. They should not accept anything blindly and easily. They must find the truth by exerting themselves through trial and error, through critical judgement and penetrating study. In short, he became a great arguer and an excessive debater. He said Allah had given him excessively the faculty of reasoning and argumentation.

Soon he became a famous scholar and great philosopher. At this time Nizam al-Mulk was the Prime Minister of Malik Shah, the Seljuq Sultan, who used to summon assemblies and debates between scholars and philosophers and others of the intellectual elite. The enlightened assembly used to be entertained by al-Ghazzali's power of reasoning and his far-reaching knowledge. After the death of Imam al-Haramayn in 1091, the Prime Minister appointed al-Ghazzali, at the age of 34, as the Principal of Nizamiyya Madrasah. The people of Baghdad were enthralled by al-Ghazzali's lectures, his penetrating analysis of religion and by his clear and straightforward presentation of solutions to several difficult matters of religion. He soon became their hero. He gained wealth as well as fame. He became the Imam of the whole of Iraq and Khurasan.

He was the principal of the Nizamiyya Madrasa for only four years. But during this time his fame and name spread far and wide; and the people of the Muslim world were full of praise for his brilliant scholarship. But suddenly, at the age of forty, when he was the undisputed leader of Baghdad, he gave up and left all his fame, name and wealth, and went away on search of the Truth in different places and locations.

The gloss of this world did not hold him back. He cut himself off implacably from its clutches and went away into the desert, in hiding, to find his Lord. He remained in hiding for ten years, far away from the distracting crowds, meditating on his Lord and the Hereafter. Like a dervish he roamed from place to place, to Syria, to

Palestine, Jerusalem, Cairo, Alexandria, etc. and also to the tombs of many distinguished *awliya'*, and to many mosques in many countries. At that time nobody would ever have thought from his wretched clothes, from his worn-out appearance and from his thin voice that this man was once the greatest scholar of Baghdad and had been rising on the highest ladder of riches and luxury. While he was in this wretched condition he found his Lord. His inner eyes opened and he found the Truth.

In 1106 he came back to Baghdad and at the request of the then Prime Minister of Baghdad he agreed to start teaching again in the Nizamiyya Madrasa. During this period he wrote his famous book *Ihya 'Ulum ad-Din*. From this book he used to deliver lectures (*khutbas*) which were so full of spiritual enlightenment and all-embracing knowledge that people used to call him the *Hujjatu'l-Islam* or the Proof of Islam. But after only two years he again left the Nizamiyya Madrasa for his home town of Tus where he spent the rest of his life.

In Tus he established a *madrasa* and *khanqah* for the Sufis. It was devotion to meditation and to the Sufi line of worship that he first learnt and he had been trained under several renowned Sufis. That was also what he chose in the end and the way he spent his final years. He became a real devotee of Allah and he used to implore his Lord for reunion with Him. At last he died, taking leave of this fleeting world at the age of 53 on 10 December 1111. It is said that on the day of his death after the morning prayer he brought his coffin and kissed it again and again and placed it by his bedside. He was buried near the grave of the poet, Firdawsi.

Al-Ghazzali is one of the greatest thinkers and geniuses the world has known. The focus of his thoughts and the principal aim of his teachings and of his learned discourses were to attract people to morality. He well realised that the society of his time was steeped in the glitter and worship of this world and hence the necessity of tremendous moral teaching and religious injunctions. He devoted most of his time and most of his writings to distracting people from the enjoyment of this world and to diverting them to the upliftment of their soul and spirit. His unique scholarship, wide experience, sharp insight, deep thinking and wonderful sense of judgement went a long way to give a direction to the then disillusioned Muslim society. And his Muslim readers and followers of his thought have gained immensely, and his writings have become universally celebrated.

But al-Ghazzali's greatest contribution was in his turning the whole spiritual world of Islam into a fine presentation of *tasawwuf*. That is to say, it is the spirit that is the most important thing in Islam. And this is what al-Ghazzali in his beautiful writings has presented to the world. He was one of the greatest philosophers and thinkers of the world, nay, great philosophers like Immanuel Kant, great thinkers and poets like Dante, Pascal, etc, drew inspiration from him. He brought religion and Sufism out from the barren Greek realm of argumentation and reasoning only, and turned them into a fertile and pleasant calling tinged with a man's love for his Lord. A man's love for his Lord is the highest form of worship, and the greater his love, the greater is he as a Muslim.

His thoughts and great writings were instrumental in giving a clear direction to the disillusioned Muslims of the Middle Ages, particularly the intelligentsia of that period who were greatly influenced by Greek philosophy and by the cursed Mu'tazilite interpretation of Islam. His scholarly and high philosophical discussions and exquisite analysis of the spirit made Sufism a very attractive form of worship to the intellectual world; and the common people were also drawn very closely to Sufism. He fought against the votaries of dry reasoning and argumentation and he persuaded the strict *Shari'a* followers to see the beauty of Sufism in Islam.

He was proclaimed a reviver of Islam and the gratified Muslims greeted him as the *Hujjatu'l-Islam*, i.e. the Witness of Islam. It was owing to his influence and writings that the Muslim world got its rightful place back in the intellectual circles of the world and in the world of science and philosophy. And he did all this by drawing only from the Qur'an. Henceforth the *'ulama'* and the Sufis did not clash; they were riding on the same boat. The coordination between the two was made complete through him.

His thoughts and influence were felt, not only in the Islamic world, but also in the Christian world. The Christian world was also divided and was faced with the challenge of a spiritual vacuum because of too much exposure to philosophical arguments and arid debate. But al-Ghazzali's sharp writings and counter-arguments removed several of their misgivings as well. Thomas Aquinas (1225-1274), Dante, Raymond Martin (died 1284), Pascal, etc, were all vociferous proponents of al-Ghazzali's presentation of counter-arguments and examples. They freely accepted his arguments and applied them to their own life and religion.

Al-Ghazzali's biggest contribution was his *Ihya' 'Ulum ad-Din*, that is, *The Revival of the Knowledges of Religion*. It is divided into four volumes and each volume is divided into ten chapters. In the analysis of the most delicate matters of religion, and in high scholarship, this book is one of the greatest masterpieces of the world. A famous writer of the thirteenth century, an-Nawawi, observed about this book that if all writings ceased to exist, the *Ihya' 'Ulum ad-Din* alone would be enough. Several Sufis treat it as being next to the Qur'an and *Sunna.* His other books, *Tahafut al-Falasifa, Fatihatu'l-'Ulum,* and *al-I'tiqad* were his great contributions to philosophy. His several other spiritual books like *Rawda at-Talibin, al-Ma'arif al-'Aqila, ar-Risala al-Laduniya* etc were books of a very high order in spiritual matters. His *Kimiya as-Sa'ada* is another incommensurate book like the *Ihya' 'Ulum ad-Din,* and is full of high scholarship and high intellectual discussion in the light of the Qur'an and *Sunna.*

He also wrote many poems. His poems are faithfully and religiously recited by Sufis all over the world. He was also a great lover of songs. But only songs that enlivened the spirit. He said, "The purpose of songs is to inspire the spirit to love of Allah, and the song which can inspire the listener to the love of Allah is the real song."

17
'Abdu'l-Qadir al-Jilani (1077-1165)

Who are more wrong than those who forge a lie against Allah or deny His signs? Never will such wrong people prosper. (Qur'an 10:17)

'Abdu'l-Qadir al-Jilani is one of those scholars and geniuses who came to this earth to give light to humanity and guide them to the true path. He practised Islam and conveyed its message to all Muslims after having himself drunk deeply from the hearts of humanity. The place where he lived and chose for the spread of his message has become one of the blessed lands on this earth, and has since been turned into a blessed centre of visits by his followers and well-wishers.

It is very difficult to give a correct evaluation of his personality because several of his followers have given descriptions of his life and personality. Some have painted him as one of the greatest Sufis, rather the greatest Sufi, and have alleged that he performed several unheard-of *karamat*, or miracles, while others have described him as one of the greatest *'ulama'*, that is, scholars, of Islam. From a neutral point of view we can say he was a great reformer, a great idealist, a great scholar, a great preacher of Islam and a great Sufi. His unbounded scholarship of Islam was so great that the great Moorish scholar and philosopher, Ibn al-'Arabi gave him the title of *Qutb.* that is, the focal point of Islam.

In the sixth century AH, Muslim civilization, under the lavish rule of the Abbasid khalifate, was going under, and the Muslims in general were losing their attachment to religion. There was real moral bankruptcy and the people were indulging in luxury and the pleasures of this life. However, in the background there was a reign of corruption, a reign of injustice and a world of indiscipline. People were steeped in irreligious activities and there was hardly any regard for moral scruples. From the Khalif to the common man, all had gone away from religion.

Under this extreme decline of morality 'Abdu'l-Qadir al-Jilani used to stand up boldly to address the people to remind them of their moral responsibility. The Khalif, the *qadis*, the governors, the public, the merchants, the *'ulama'* - all sections of people were the target of his addresses or *khutbas*. He would criticise their defects and shortcomings very boldly and would suggest the measures and remedies of the Qur'an and *Sunna*. At first his voice was hardly heard and his audience very small, about ten or fifteen people. But gradually, in the course of time, his audience became sixty to seventy thousand people. They would listen to him with all their heart and mind and would drink deep from the fountain of his scholarly lectures.

This distinguished and ever-respected scholar, Sayyid Abu Muhammad 'Abdu'l-Qadir, was born in Persia in the province of Jilan in the year 1077. He was called al-Jilani after the name of his birthplace. His father, Abu Salih, was a very religious person and a great *'alim*. Abu Salih was a descendant of Fatima's son, Hasan, and his wife was descended from her other son, Husayn.

From his boyhood, 'Abdu'l-Qadir was very calm, quiet, thoughtful and a keen seeker of knowledge. In his childhood he studied Arabic and Persian in the local *madrasa*. When he was eighteen, he was sent to Baghdad to study the Qur'an, *Hadith*, *fiqh*, theology, logic (*mantiq*), history and philosophy in the famous Nizamiyya Madrasa of Baghdad. When he was setting out for Baghdad, his mother gave him forty gold coins and hid them by sewing them in his undergarment. On the way, his caravan was attacked by bandits. When they asked him if he had anything, he showed them his forty gold coins hidden in his undergarment. The bandit leader rebuked him for having admitted this. At this 'Abdu'l-Qadir replied that this mother has asked him, when she bade him farewell, never to tell a lie, even at the risk of his life. The bandit leader, having heard this, was greatly moved, and he along with all the other bandits accepted Islam and vowed to live an honest life henceforward.

Having reached Baghdad, 'Abdu'l-Qadir started swimming in the ocean of knowledge of the Qur'an, *hadith*, *fiqh*, and other related subjects. Soon he showed his genius as an excellent student by dint of his sharp memory and deep understanding. But he was more attracted to the spiritual side of learning, and Sufism made its full impact on him. Side by side with his studies in the Nizamiyya Madrasa he freely mixed with all the renowned Sufis of his time in Baghdad. In this way he got very closely acquainted with the famous Sufi of Baghdad, Hammad, who accepted him as one of his favourite disciples.

He dedicated himself to attaining the depths of Sufism by his constant devotion and association with the Sufis. After his studies were over, he preferred to live in loneliness away from the public, and to meditate on his Lord. He took on a strict and rigorous life of abstinence and austerity and used to spend his nights in prayer and meditation. He would complete one reading of the Qur'an, almost every night, by keeping himself awake;

and it is said that with one *wudu'* (ablution) he used to say the *'Isha'* and *Fajr* prayers. Then he left Baghdad and went to a lonely desert where he spent twenty-five years in meditation and self-purification. At that time he had the look of an ascetic, unworldly, man. The goal of this long course of Sufi self-purification was to know his Lord and he was successful in his quest.

At the age of 51, he came back to Baghdad, to be among people again, and started preaching the message of Islam at the instigation of the Sufi, Yusuf al-Hamadani. People started gathering round him in groups, and gradually in thousands. They accepted his leadership. On every Wednesday night he used to give his addresses at a local open space and people from all walks of life thronged to him. They would listen to him spell-bound and would correct themselves as he directed and prescribed. But the assembly gradually grew unmanageable. The open space had to be widened and additional place provided for accommodating the tens of thousands of his audience and disciples. A large guest house was built for visitors.

The name of 'Abdu'l-Qadir al-Jilani was on the tongues of all the people of Baghdad and his discourses were the topic of their conversation. He portrayed the glory of Islam in a new light and presented this glory with new splendour in the light of the Qur'an and *Sunna,* in such convincing language and with such spirit, that people in thousands became his disciples. They gave him the title of *Muhyiddin,* that is, the Reviver of Islam. His tens of thousands of followers consisted of Sufis, *fuqaha,* *'ulama'*, ministers, the Khalif and the common people. And they all used to get equal treatment from him. His dedication, his struggles, his self-purification and his total submission to Allah attracted all people and earned him the nickname of *Ghawth al-A'zam*, that is, the Chief of all the Sufis.

'Abdu'l-Qadir in his ripe old age married four wives and was blessed with twenty-seven sons and twenty-two daughters. His family life was very calm and peaceful. He used to fast the entire year except for five days. He would give *khutbas* and *fatwas* during the day and would meditate for the entire night. This was his usual practice. Only after the *Maghrib* prayer would he eat, together with all the beggars and destitutes around him, joining in the same meal. In this way he spent his life in the service of Islam and humanity, and died at the age of ninety-one. Millions of his followers belonging to his *Tariqa Qadariya* still actively remember him and celebrate the anniversary of his death.

From his *khutbas* and messages, anthologists have succeeded in collecting a comprehensive anthology under the title of *Futuh al-Ghayb* or *The Openings from the Unseen*. Apart from this, another anthology of his *khutbas, al-Fath ar-Rabbani* and an anthology of poems are said to be of very superior literary and spiritual merit. They speak of his deep insight into the spiritual world as well as of his profound sympathy for people and for all the creatures of Allah. His knowledge of this world and of the spirit is unbounded. His scholarship of the Qur'an and *Sunna* was both intensive and extensive and his self-purification and sacrifices for the cause of his Lord were truly remarkable. It is for this that Allah has granted him the honour of the title of *Ghawth al-A'dham* and the title of *Muhyiddin*.

He was undoubtedly one of the greatest *'ulama'* of the world and one of the greatest scholars of Islam. He is said to have written more than forty books on Islam, but unfortunately none of these invaluable books is available in any library of the world. It is quite possible that during the Hülügü holocaust in Baghdad in 1258 all these books were burnt along with the destruction of the historic city.

He was against worldly fame and the glitter of this world. He used to declare that those who said that they worshipped Allah, but were in fact hankering after the wealth and fame of this world, were, in fact, worshippers of this world. They worshipped their *qadis* and governors; they worshipped their local chieftains; and thus worshipping they lost their entire life. They had no time to worship Allah. The fear of these semi-lords was always upperhand in their hearts. And this fear was caused by their greed for the fame and wealth of this world. Once greed for this world was gone, they would be in a fitting position to owe their total submission and unbounded allegiance to their Lord. He used to say there was no place for several lords on the Throne of Allah. A true Muslim must clear himself of all these semi-lords.

He was also of the opinion that a Muslim's prayer, fasting, *hajj*, etc. were nothing if they did not help him come closer to his Lord. That is to say, he must do all these things with such devotion and obedience that his Lord would be pleased to raise him up. He must feel that his Lord was pleased with him and he must feel His presence everywhere. He must not be "a beggar for fame," rather he must be "a beggar for His mercy," he used to declare.

He also used to rebuke those who would sit in idleness and blame their fate. He said that only those who were idle would have time to refer to their fate. A Muslim should go on doing his duty and the result would be up to Allah.

'Abdu'l-Qadir al-Jilani with his profound knowledge of the Qur'an and *Sunna* and with his limitless belief in Allah and by his countless sacrifices and struggles, served his people and his Lord. Indeed he deserved to be called the *Ghawth al-A'dham*.

18
'Umar Khayyam (1028-1123)

As to those who hold fast by the Book and establish regular prayer, never shall We allow the reward of the righteous to perish. (Qur'an 7:170)

For about four or five hundred years from the seventh to the eleventh century AD, the Muslim renaissance in the field of knowledge and science was at its peak, and the contributions made by Muslim scholars and thinkers to the world at large ushered in an era of a glorious and refreshing Muslim art and culture. Then after the middle of the eleventh century there was a big decline of this glorious era (of art and culture) in the face of stiff opposition from anti-progressive forces. Along with this decline there was a profound lull in scientific and other educational pursuits. The Muslim era of knowledge and science started declining.

At this critical juncture a great scientist, astronomer, astrologer and a passionate and versatile poet, 'Umar Khayyam, appeared on the scene and started reviving the declining era of scholarship and scientific pursuits. His full name was Abu'l-Fath 'Umar ibn Ibrahim al-Khayyami. He was known as a poet of rationality and reasoning, but he was also a great mathematician and a famous astronomer.

His life and genealogy are shrouded in all kinds of mysterious and wondrous descriptions given by his numerous infatuated followers. Historians have had to grope in the darkness even to find the dates of his birth and death. Even the great biographer, Ibn Khalliqan, and his follower, Ibn Shakir, are silent about him. At any rate, from various booklets and reference sources, whatever information was available has been deciphered by his biographers in the following manner:

He was born between 1038 and 1048 in Nishapur. His parents were traders in the tent business, and that is why he was known as Khayyam which means tent merchant. His father gave him a proper education and training and sent him to a famous institution of Nishapur for his studies. According to many biographers, he was a class-fellow of the Seljuqi Prime Minister, Azam al-Mulk, who promised him to take care of him when he was in power.

'Umar was from his boyhood a keen and meritorious student. His memory was unusually sharp. He could memorise any difficult lesson or book, and once he learnt something he would never forget it. It is said that once, in Isfahan, he studied a large arithmetical book seven times and when he returned to Nishapur he reproduced the whole book from his memory without any mistake. He had unusual command of the languages of Persian and Arabic. He was a good reciter of the Qur'an and he could recite the Qur'an in the seven approved recensions. He had great knowledge of philosophy, arithmetic, astrology and astronomy. He used to acknowledge Ibn Sina as his mentor and he drew inspiration from Ibn Sina's thoughts and philosophy.

After his studies were completed, he took up teaching as a lecturer in the Nishapur College and soon he became famous as a mathematician and as an astronomer. When his name and fame reached the ears of Nizam al-Mulk, the Seljuq Prime Minister, and the King, Malik Shah, he was appointed in the King's court as an astronomer.

Malik Shah, the King, was keenly interested in astronomy, and that is why he established a famous observatory in Nishapur and appointed 'Umar Khayyam as its chief. 'Umar Khayyam and his colleagues worked hard for several years in this observatory and succeeded in producing the *Tarikh al-Jalali* calendar. This calendar was, in many respects, better than the Gregorian calendar produced in 1582 by Pope Gregory in Rome.

'Umar Khayyam became a very close friend of the Prime Minister, Nizam al-Mulk, and the King, Malik Shah. Both of them used to respect him and treat him as a confidant. When in 1092 they were both killed by assassins, 'Umar Khayyam was deeply shocked and retired from the King's court and went to Nishapur College where he re-started his career as a lecturer once more. After about eight to ten years' more service, he retired from the college, but he was surrounded every day by numerous seekers of knowledge who came to consult him and to seek his mature opinion on many matters. He died in Nishapur at the age of over 80.

A famous writer, Nizam-i al-'Arudi, wrote that once, in 1112-13, he visited 'Umar Khayyam in a friend's house in Balkh when 'Umar Khayyam remarked that his grave would be covered with flowers at least twice a year. He was surprised at this prophecy. But twenty-four years later, in 1136, the writer had the chance to go to Nishapur and happened to visit 'Umar Khayyam's grave on a Friday night, he found, to his great astonishment, that the grave was completely covered with beautiful flowers.

'Umar Khayyam was undoubtedly a great philosopher, a great mathematician and a great astronomer. He wrote in Arabic more than ten books on philosophy, astronomy and mathematics. Of them his famous book, *al-Jibr*, is his greatest contribution to the world of knowledge. In this book, he showed his real scholarship and originality. The famous algebra writer, Al-Khwarizmi, did not show more originality and scholarship than he in solving the many problems of algebra and geometry. In 1857, Woepeke edited and translated Khayyam's book *Al-Jibr*. His other book on geometry was a great improvement of Euclid's book on the same subject, and it showed his high scholarship and splendid originality.

But 'Umar Khayyam has remained most famous for his powerful and beautiful quatrains, the *Ruba'iyat*. He was a poet of great excellence. His beautiful verses have moved poets of both the West and the East. The writers and poets of his age did not and could not give him adequate recognition, but six centuries later an accomplished poet of the West, Fitzgerald, came out boldly to sing the songs of 'Umar Khayyam, and he translated a good many of his couplets.

It is very difficult to determine the number of poems and verses that 'Umar Khayyam composed, but the number of *Ruba'iyat*, that is, the quatrains, is more than twelve hundred. However there are many claimants to the composition of these, and nobody is absolutely sure who actually composed them. But they were passed on as the *Ruba'iyat-i 'Umar Khayyam*.

'Umar Khayyam was undoubtedly a great mystic poet, a great monotheistic writer, extremely rational and an extremely argumentative poet. He was opposed to the orthodox *'ulama'* and was opposed to all institutionalised regulations of religion. To him several institutions of religion were meaningless. Sufism was uncalled-for, and excessive fervour for religion was something detested. He was for natural religion and for a natural and humanitarian approach to it. His *Ruba'iyat* were for a clean and simple man. He was for forgiveness of man for all his errors and his sympathy went deep into his heart.

But above all he was an optimist and not a pessimist. To him beauty, truth, life, welfare had a special appeal. He was for all humanity. But he believed in the transmigration of souls which is against the fundamental beliefs of Islam. And that is why orthodox Muslims have never accepted him as a poet of Islam.

19
Ibn Rushd (1126 - 1198)

Those who rest not their hopes on their meeting with Us and are pleased and satisfied with the life of this world are those who heed not Our signs. (Qur'an 10:7)

The Middle Ages the Muslim philosophers of Baghdad and Andalus (Muslim Spain) made their greatest contribution by presenting a balanced system of thought, combining Greek and Islamic philosophy. In this work, al-Kindi, al-Farabi and Ibn Sina were in the forefront. A contemporary of them was Ibn Rushd of Spain who of all the Muslim philosophers made the greatest impact on European philosophy. In the history of Europe he is known as Averroes.

Abu'l-Walid Muhammad ibn Ahmad ibn Muhammad ibn Rushd was born in Cordoba in 1126. His forefathers in Cordoba had established themselves as *fuqaha'* for several generations. His father and grandfather were *qadis* in Cordoba. His grandfather, al-Murabid, was the Chief Justice of all Andalusia.

In childhood Ibn Rushd received his education in Cordoba. He studied the Qur'an, *hadith, fiqh,* literature, mathematics, astronomy, philosophy, logic, history, etc. He also learnt Greek and Hebrew very thoroughly. Those from al-Kindi to Ibn Sina who had studied Aristotle and Plato and had written books on them were first studied by Ibn Rushd very keenly so that he was acquainted with them. His habit of study was such that he used to read sixteen hours a day even when he 70. It is said that he left no book of any prominent author unread. He even used to make notes on each book he read.

Very soon he made his name as a philosopher, a debater, a *faqih*, and as a physician. Most of the prominent physicians of Andalus used to visit him to acquaint themselves with his medical treatments. At 40 he confined himself almost exclusively to *fiqh* and philosophy and surprised all his contemporaries by his unusual proficiency in these two subjects. In 1169 he became *qadi* at Seville and two years later he became *qadi* at Cordoba. He remained the *Qadi* of Cordoba for twelve years and made a name as a good jurisprudent, but this occupation disturbed his studies and attainment of knowledge.

In 1172, Ibn Rushd, at the instance of his friend and fellow philosopher and physician, Ibn Tufayl, became the royal physician to the Moroccan sultan, Abu Ya'qub Yusuf. After the death of Abu Ya'qub Yusuf, al-Mansur made him again the royal physician and accepted him as one of his closest friends. His reputation, fame and wealth under the patronage of al-Mansur increased manifold and people all around became extremely jealous of him. The *'ulama'* and the *fuqaha'* of the country became antagonistic towards him and spread a rumour that Ibn Rushd did not believe in the Qur'an as the word of Allah and that therefore he was not a Muslim. At the instigation of the orthodox *'ulama'* the common people also became very hostile towards him and they called him a *munafiq*, i.e. a hypocrite.

Al-Mansur became very perturbed at this development and eventually was forced to banish him from the country. Ibn Rushd returned to his birthplace, Cordoba, and lived in peace. Meanwhile, al-Mansur was made aware of the conspiracy of the *'ulama'* and he recalled Ibn Rushd to Morocco and reinstated him in his old place. But Ibn Rushd by then was already broken in health and he died very shortly thereafter at the age of 72 on 10 December 1198, and was buried in Cordoba.

Nobody can say accurately the number of books which Ibn Rushd wrote, but his books are many and are of historic importance. He wrote principally on jurisprudence, medical science and philosophy. He also made critical analyses of astronomy, mathematics, grammar and philology. Several of his manuscripts are still available and several of his books have been translated into German and other European languages. Before the end of the twelfth century most of his prominent books were translated into Latin and were being published along with Aristotle's books on philosophy. He wrote three major works on Aristotle - *Jami'*, an abridged edition, *Takhlis*, an introduction, and *Sharha*, i.e. detailed explanation.

He wrote a rejoinder to Imam al-Ghazzali's *Tahafut al-Falasifa* in his book called *Tahafut at-Tahafut, The Incoherence of the Incoherence*, negating al-Ghazzali's attempt to prove the incoherence of the philosophers. In this book he showed his sharp reasoning power, high scholarship, and pointed criticism verging on cleverness. It was for this book he was attacked by the *'ulama'*.

Ibn Rushd also wrote several books on medical science. *Kulliyat fi't-Tibb* is a famous book on medicine and the doctors and *hakims* of subsequent periods used to consult it regularly. There are detailed discussions in this book on different diseases, their symptoms and remedies. It is in this book that he pointed out that smallpox never repeated itself in the same patient. He also translated Ibn Sina's medical book *Urjuja* and wrote eighteen more booklets on the subject of medicine.

But the philosopher Ibn Rushd was more recognised in the world than the physician Ibn Rushd. His books on philosophy had a far-reaching effect on European philosophers. For several centuries until the Renaissance his theories and conclusions on several philosophical issues were the main guidelines, together with those of Aristotle. Many scholars regarded him as the father of Western philosophy. It was Michael Scotus through his translation of Ibn Rushd's books and theories in 1250 AD who was responsible for introducing Aristotle, for the first time, thoroughly, to the West. Even if he was lost to the Arab world, he was very much alive in the Latin world. Researchers have now, of course, found out after studying his essays thoroughly, that he was not in any way an unbeliever; but both the Islamic world and the Christian world at that time branded him as an atheist. The Christian Church in Paris had to issue a declaration, containing 219 references condemning his "Averroism".

However, in spite of this Europe, had no other alternative but to include his versions of philosophical conclusions in the curricula of their universities. The influential University of Padua became of the centre of Averroism. Many scholars in Europe made their names by writing theses on Averroism. In Oxford he was established as the interpreter of Aristotle. Francis Bacon honoured him as being a mid-point between Aristotle and Ibn Sina and he advised all to study his essays in Arabic to avoid the faulty translations.

Ibn Rushd placed intellect above everything else. In doing so, he was following Aristotle. Rather he surpassed Aristotle in over-emphasizing the intellect. He tried to correlate the intellect with revelation failing to distinguish between the two. He thought an intellectual man was capable of experiencing revelation and that there was hardly any distinction between revelation and intellect. This was an error and he was branded by both the Church and the *'ulama'* as an agnostic.

Like several so-called "intellectual giants" in the West and in the East, Ibn Rushd wanted to judge everything, including revelation, by the standard of human intellect. The fact that the human intellect is imperfect and capable of reaching, at times, wrong decisions and conclusions was forgotten by him. The Qur'an says, *"You have been given but a very little knowledge."* (Qur'an 17:85) Man has not been given complete knowledge of everything. So how can he equate his intellect with revelation which is sent down by the Perfect and Omnipotent Allah? Those who try to equate the two are far from truth and are in danger of agnosticism.

Ibn Rushd wanted to justify the revelation of the Qur'an through his intellect and philosophical reasoning. He did not reject the revelation nor did he minimise the nature of prophethood or miracles. His latest biographer, the French scholar, Renan, tells us that there was no evidence, whatsoever, to say that Ibn Rushd was an atheist. His belief in Islam, till his last days, says Al-Ansari, Abdu'l-Wali and other biographers, was intact.

His political beliefs were that man must be free from all oppression and injustice. He used to believe in Plato's ideas of social order. He also believed that the rule of the *Khulafa' ar-Rashidun* was the ideal rule for humanity, and that it was Mu'awiya who made the greatest blunder by introducing dictatorship.

20
Shaykh Sa'di (1184 - 1291)

Those who rest not their hopes on their meeting with Us and are pleased and satisfied with the life of this world are those who heed not Our Signs. (Qur'an 10:7)

Once in a flower garden in Iran, a thoughtful poet perceived that a friend of his was exceedingly preoccupied with a bunch of flowers and had no time to look at anything else. The poet asked him what it was that captivated him so much in these flowers which were sure to fade before sunset. His friend replied by asking him what could possibly replace the beauty of flowers. The poet said, "For people like you who are attracted to the beauty of flowers whose life-span is at most five or six days, I will write a book called the *Gulistan* (garden of flowers) which will last indefinitely."

The name of the poet was Shaykh Muslihuddin Sa'di and he was born in Shiraz in Persia in the year 1184 AD. His father 'Abdullah was a descendent of 'Ali and was nobleman in the service of the court of 'Ata Beg Tughal. Sa'di lost his parents early in his life and so he fell into poverty. His elder brother somehow managed to keep the family by owning a fruit shop.

Sa'di's life consisted of three periods. Until 1226 he was busy with his studies. From 1226 to 1256, he spent his life as a traveller in different countries of the world. And the last part from 1256 - 1291 he spent in hirazwriting, contemplating and admonishing people as a Sufi.

In those days Shiraz was a great centre of learning and Sa'di was admitted into a big *madrasa* there where he received his primary education. Then he left for higher education in the famous Nizamiyya Madrasa of Baghdad. He studied philosophy and science under the able guidance of Farah Ibn al-Jawahir. Then he studied logic, history, geography, philosophy, *tafsir, hadith, fiqh*, etc. He was very religious from his boyhood and he was a strict follower of the *Shari'a*. While in Baghdad he received extensive instruction in *tasawwuf* (sufism) from several Sufis that he came in contact with and became a follower of the famous Sufi Shaykh Shihabu'd-din as-Suhrawardi (died 1234) whose influence and association had a great impact on him. Sa'di was a master of several languages but he wrote only in his mother tongue, Persian, and occasionally in Arabic.

After the end of his studies in Baghdad he came back to Shiraz, but found that his chief patron Sultan Ata Beg had been killed by the Khwarizmi Sultan, Ghiyathu'd-din Isfahani. Following this political upset the general people were subjected to looting and exploitation by the Mongols and Turks, and their miseries knew no bounds. Seeing their misery, he found the situation unbearable and he left the country and decided to go on travelling from country to country.

From 1226-1256, for a period of thirty years, he travelled from Shiraz to Khurasan, to Tatar, to Balkh, to Kashghar, Ghazna, Punjab, Somnath, Gujarat, Yemen, Hijaz, Abyssinia, Palestine, Syria, Damascus, Ba'albek, North Africa, Asia Minor, etc. In each of these places he stayed for months or years, studied the people and gained many and varied experiences. While in Somnath, he saw the idol worship of the Hindus and recorded his astonishing experiences in the *Bustan* in beautiful couplets. From Somnath he went to Gujarat, and then to

Punjab and then to Delhi. From Delhi he went to the Yemen where he lost his son by his first wife. He was very upset at this loss.

From the Yemen he went to Abyssinia where he took part in a *jihad* against the Christians. Then he went to Makka and performed the *Hajj*. In all, he performed *Hajj* fourteen times on foot. From Makka to went to Damascus and then Ba'albek. In Damascus and Ba'albek he started giving sermons on religion and people gave him the title of Shaykh. His lectures and sermons were received with great appreciation. Then he left for Jerusalem and for some time he hid himself in a lonely place far from other people. At this time, he fell into the hands of Frankish soldiers who arrested him and sent him to Tripoli to work as as an ordinary prisoner digging ditches. He experienced how painful the life of a prisoner was and was forced to spend some time in this inhuman life in captivity.

At last a friend of his from Aleppo got him released on payment of a large ransom and also gave him his daughter in marriage. However this wife was very hot-tempered and ill-spoken. He could not bear her and had to leave Aleppo and Asia Minor and finally ending his journeying in his birthplace, Shiraz, in the year 1256.

In Shiraz his old patron, Sultan Ata Beg, had been succeeded by his son Sultan Abu Bakr. The conditions of people had also changed for the better. At the request of Sultan Abu Bakr and his other friends he decided to stay on permanently in Shiraz and to devote his time to the meditation on Allah and to his writings. He was by then an old man but very rich and mature with a wealth of experience gained by thirty years of travel over a great part of the world. The books he now produced were so rich a fountain that people have been drinking ever since from them with no sign of satiety. The *Bustan* and the *Gulistan* have maintained their popularity right up until the present day.

At the time he was engaged in writing his *Bustan* and *Gulistan*, he was already past eighty and his mind was at its purest. He was above any small things or demands of this world. He was completely devoted to his Lord portraying Him as *Jamil*^{un} *Karim*^{un} *Rahman*^{ur} *Rahim* and His Prophet as his *shafi'*^{un}, *qasim*^{un} *Jasmin*^{un} *Nasim*^{un}. The great contribution that Shaykh Sa'di made to the Islamic world lies in his two great couplets, famous equally in the Arab and non-Arab world, on the person of the Prophet, and which are read with equal zeal and fervour by both Arabs and non-Arabs. They are:

Balaghal ula bi-kamalihi
Kashafad-duja bi-jamalihi
Hasanath jami'u khisalihi
Sallu 'alayhi wa alihi

These two couplets are in the mouth of every Muslim, boy or girl, man or woman, young or old. They are the best epithet, the best eulogy, and the best offering that a human being can offer to the Prophet who does not need any praise from any of us because his Lord has promised him complete satisfaction and has conferred on him the title of *Rahmat al-'alamin*.

Shaykh Sa'di died at the ripe age of 110 in the year 1291 AD in Shiraz and was buried there, where later the poet Hafiz was also buried. His grave bears no extraordinary monument except an epitaph of a few couplets from his *Bustan*, the first couplets of which are:

O traveller! You have stepped on my dust.
Beware!
You have to remember me for the sake of
the Almighty's dust.
Sa'di will certainly be buried in dust
Because he was like dust while he lived.
(*Bustan*)

Sa'di wrote mostly in poetry except for the *Risala* which is in six volumes, a few chapters of the *Gulistan* and a part of the *Khubisat* in prose. All his other writings were in beautiful Persian verse. He wrote his *Qasidas* in both Arabic and Persian. He wrote his some of his *Mirasi* (Odes on Sorrow) in Persian and some in Arabic. All his other *ghazals, ruba'iyat* and *qasidas* were written in Persian. His *ghazals,* if not perfect like those of Hafiz, were full of common sense and common appeal, rich with morals and ethics, tasteful, discerning, and entertaining and full of common sense.

In the Islamic world, particularly in the East, nobody is considered literate and cultured if he does not quote from Sa'di. The famous Sufi poet, 'Abdu'r-Rahman Jami' (14114-1492), says, "The intellectual world calls Sa'di's *ghazals* a salt cup, but for centuries, the educated people of the East have been committing to their memory Sa'di's *ghazals* and have been accepting his morals and ethics as their ideal."

Sa'di's *Mirasi,* (Odes on Sorrow) started with the death of Abu Bakr Sa'd and ended with the tragic death of the Khalif Mu'tasim and the destruction of the city of Baghdad by the Mongol hordes of Hülügü in 1258. Sa'di's favourite Nizamiyya Madrasa was destroyed along and he could not control his emotion and anger at this dastardly act of the cruellest looter and plunderer in the history of the world. He termed this destruction the Day of the Destruction of the World, and he implored the Prophet Muhammad to rise and to see this destruction. Eight hundred thousand people were said to have been massacred, leaving not a single soul alive in Baghdad; and all the buildings, palaces, libraries, universities, *madrasas*, hospitals, etc. were razed to the ground, effacing totally five hundred years of Muslim civilization that had been built up in Baghdad.

Shaykh Sa'di is one of the greatest travellers of the East like al-Mas'udi, Ibn Haykal, and Ibn Battuta. He, of course, did not write his travels and experiences like them, but he gave his full might and the whole weight of his gathered experience over the years in his *Gulistan* and *Bustan*. And that is why he is remembered in Persian literature as a great moralist whose morals are in everybody's mouth.

He is considered a great essayist and the best portrayer of human weaknesses. His examples and presentations are superb. Some examples are:

(1) A short-statured wise man is better than a giant who is ignorant.

(2) A sheep may be small but its meat is tasty while an elephant is big, but its meat is not food.

(3) Of all mountains Sinai is the smallest, but its place is the best to Allah.

(4) One small Arab horse is better than a herd of donkeys.

(5) It is better to walk bare-footed than to have shoes with nails in them, and it is better to roam the streets

than to hear the nagging of a wife in the house.

21
Mawlana Jalalu'd-din Rumi (1207 - 1273)

O you who believe, betray not the trust of Allah and His Messenger, nor misappropriate knowingly things entrusted to you. (Qur'an 8:27)

The Muslims believe that the Qur'an is the word of Allah and no other book by any human being can compare with the Book of Allah. But Persian-speakingMuslims regard the *Mathnawi* of Mawlana Jalalu'd-din Rumi as almost the Qur'an in the Persian language. Mawlana Jalalu'd-din Rumi was born on 30 September 1207 in Balkh in the province of Khurasan. He was descended from Abu Bakr as-Siddiq on his father's side, and on his mother's side he was descended from Khurasan's ruler, Khwarizm Shah. Although he was born and brought up in Central Asia, and although he had Turkish blood in his veins and spent almost fifty years in Konya, a Turkish city, he never wrote anything in Turkish.

His grandfather, Mawlana Husayn Balkhi and his father Mawlana Bahi'ud-din Balkhi were both great scholars of Islam and were highly regarded by people as great *'ulama'*. While was a child, his father Mawlana Baha'ud-din had a disagreement with the ruler of Khurasan and in consequence was forced to leave Khurasan and to roam for fifteen or sixteen years from Nishapur to Baghdad, Makka, Malata, Larinda, etc. Ultimately, he settled down in Konia the capital of a small principality of Asia Minor which had been part of the Roman empire. From this connection he took his nickname, Rumi.

While staying in Nishapur he came into contact with the famous Sufi, Faridu'd-din 'Attar (died 26 April 1230) who presented him with his great book *Asrarnamè* and who prophesied that Jalalu'd-din would one day be a great man. While he was in Larinda he married a Turkish woman by whom he had two sons and then she died. He later married another wife.

Although his childhood was somewhat turbulent he had no break in his studies. His father taught him *tafsir, fiqh, hadith, 'ilm al-kalam,* history, philosophy, etc. Besides this, his father also gave him his first instruction in *tasawwuf*. He had a retentive memory and great intelligence. He never lost his love for learning. He was also an ardent follower and student of religion, and he attained substantial knowledge of the *Shari'a* and Sufism in his youth.

After the death of his father he devoted himself to attaining the high stages of Sufism from his father's disciple, Burhanu'd-din Muhaqqiq. Then he went to the universities of Aleppo and Damascus to acquire further knowledge on different subjects. After the death of his Master, Burhanu'd-din, he became a Shaykh and people from all walks of life in Konia came to visit him. He spent his time writing, lecturing and giving instruction in *tasawwuf*. In several difficult and acute problems of the *Shari'a,* it was he who give the correct solutions and interpretations. All his contemporaries among the *'ulama'* bore no comparison with him.

In the early part of his life he was a very conservative and orthodox Muslim. He was very much opposed to art, songs, dancing, etc. in the name of religion. But after he came in contact with his spiritual mentor, Shams-i Tabriz, he was a changed man. He became a great lover of religious songs and dances, and he introduced *sama*, a kind of religious song performed with refrains .

He was a great lover of books and literature, and used to remain deeply occupied with them. Seeing his deep absorption, his shaykh-to-be, Shams-i Tabriz, one day asked him what he was engaged in. He replied that these were high philosophical books which he would not understand. At this the shaykh seized the pile of books and threw them into a well where they sank. The Mawlana became very angry at this and he asked Shams if he understood how great a loss he had caused him. Without any further exchange of words his shaykh pulled out the books from the depths of the water and he found that none of the pages was wet. Upon witnessing this miracle he became very much moved and at once submitted to Shams with all his heart and became his disciple.

From then on the teacher-student relationship became so deep that the Mawlana's family, his other relations, and his followers became alarmed, and it is said that they conspired to have the shaykh killed in secret. At the untimely death of his Master, Mawlana Rumi broke down. He cut off all relations with the world and engaged himself in meditation on Allah, and in writing books on Sufism. At this time, one of his disciples named Salahu'd-din used to take down copies of his poems, and after his death, Hushamu'd-din, became the Mawlana's special disciple and was the copyist of *Mathnawi*. Mawlana died at the age of 69 on 17th December 1273 and was buried in Konya. At his death the entire Muslim world was stunned, and all people, Muslims, Jews, Christians, all felt the loss. One Christian was heard chanting the words, "He was our Moses and David and he was our Jesus and we were his followers."

He was very amiable in nature and very mild in disposition. All people irrespective of age, race or colour used to love and respect him. Children were particularly attracted to him. He did not take favours from anybody. He was called the *Sultan as-Sufi*, the King of Sufis, and he performed several miracles to the wonderment of his innumerable followers and the public.

The three most famous great Sufis in the Muslim world are Imam al-Ghazzali, Shaykh al-Akbar Ibn al-'Arabi and Mawlana Jalalu'd-din Rumi. The three greatest poets known for their mysticism are Hakim Sana'i, Faridu'd-din 'Attar and Mawlana Rumi. Mawlana Rumi accepted both Sana'i and 'Attar as his preceptors in Sufism.

But Mawlana Rumi was, above all, a great thinker, a great scholar and a great Muslim reformer. His contribution to the world of literature is unique, and he is regarded as one of the greatest scholars of the world.

Of his writings, *Diwan-i-Shams-i Tabriz*, the *Mathnawi* and the *Ruba'iyat* are the greatest. Besides these he wrote an anthology of letters, *Fihi ma Fihi*, addressed to one of his dearest disciples, Mu'inu'd-din, in which he admonished him with lucid reasoning on religion, ethics and on other social and spiritual values. *Diwan-i-Shams-i Tabrizi* contains approximately two and a half thousand *ghazals* which were dedicated to his spiritual master, Shams-i Tabriz, highlighting his ideals and teachings. His *Ruba'iyat* has more than sixteen thousand *ghazals* which were full of spiritual ideals.

His greatest contribution to the world of literature and to the world of Islam, however, is his *Mathnawi*. It is written in six volumes having more twenty-five thousand couplets or *ghazals*. It is said that for forty-three years he went on meditating and adding to these *ghazals*. Towards the end of his life, he used to stay awake the whole night dictating, and his close disciple, Hushamu'd-din, used to remain with him copying his *ghazals*.

His *Mathnawi* is a mine of spiritual thoughts and a sea of knowledge about Sufism and man's spiritual possibilities. His *Diwan-i-Shams-i Tabriz* from the artistic and literary point of view is a great book, but in spiritual appeal and in the wider world of the heart and beyond, the *Mathnawi* has no parallel. It is more penetrating than the echoing songs of the mountains and more fragrant than the fragrance of flowers.

In Persian literature, the most popular books are: Firdawsi's *Shahnamè*, the *Diwan* of Hafiz, Sa'di's *Gulistan* and Rumi's *Mathnawi*. In the entire Muslim world, the importance of these four books is so great that no man is considered educated who is not acquainted with them.

In short, Rumi was a great personality, greater than any description we can give of him. He was a lover of all that is good, pure and beautiful. But, above all, he was a lover of the love of Allah. This love of Allah is the pinnacle of man's possibilities. And to reach that pinnacle of love, man's intelligence and reasoning are not sufficient. Intelligence and reasoning are very limited. It is the love of Allah that will lead him to his goal. But this should not make him forget his obligations to his country, to his society, and to the service of man. He should try to find Allah through following what is true, what is good, what is beautiful and what is good for his country and his people. In other words, through human love he can find the love of Eternity, and that is the *Siraj al-Munira*, the greatest light.

22
Imam Ibn Taymiyya (1263 - 1328)

Do men think they will be left alone on saying, "We believe," and that they will not be tested? (Qur'an 29:2)

A limited freedom of thought first crept into Islam in the second century AH during Imam Abu Hanifa's time when he encouraged people to reason things out, and in consequence of which he was called a member of the group of *Ahl ar-Ra'y,* (people of opinion). After him the Mu'tazilites took it to the extent of almost denying the revelation of the Qur'an and they judged everything from their position of over-emphasis on intellect and reasoning. The Muslim *Ummah* was on the brink of losing their faith in Allah and in the Qur'an because they started questioning whether or not the Qur'an was the word of Allah.

The Muslim *Ummah* was saved from this crisis by Imam Abu'l-Hasan al-Ash'ari and Imam al-Ghazzali who denounced the Mu'tazilites and other free thinkers in the strongest possible terms and pleaded for unqualified faith in Allah and in the Qur'an. This blind faith or unquestioned faith in Allah and in the Hereafter was later mixed up with Sufism. This Sufism was carried to another extreme, and Pir-worship crept into Islam. People started to over-emphasize the role of Pirs or Shaykhs, and they started to seek favours, even from their graves. This apparent straying of the Muslims was checked and denounced by a great scholar and Imam of the Muslim *Ummah* who was born on 22 January 1263 in Harran. At that time the Muslim world was shivering under the constant fear of the invincible Mongols who stormed Baghdad in 1258 and killed eight hundred thousand people as well as totally destroying the city with its five hundred years of civilization.

The Imam's full name was Taqi'd-din Abu'l-'Abbas Ahmad ibn 'Abdullah ibn Taymiyya. His father, 'Abdullah ibn Muhammad, fearing the oppression of the Mongols, fled to Damascus with his family and settled down there permanently. He was a follower of the Hanbali *madh-hab* and a renowned scholar of Islam, and soon he became a professor in the University of Damascus.

Ibn Taymiyya received his primary education from his able father who taught him the Qur'an, *tafsir, Hadith,* philology, philosophy, etc. He also studied for several years under the famous scholars of the time in Damascus: Zaynu'd-din al-Muqaddasi, Najmu'd-din 'Asakir and the woman scholar Zaynab bint Makki. By means of his extraordinary capacity for learning, astonishing memory, acute judgement and shrewd logic he became well-versed in almost all the subjects at a very early age, and was acknowledged by the intelligentsia of Damascus as a major scholar.

Before he was twenty, he lost his father. Thereafter he occupied his father's position as a professor of law of the Hanbali *madh-hab*. He soon made his name as a good speaker and debater on religion. Every Friday he used to give lectures on the *tafsir* of the Qur'an in the great mosque of Damascus. In spite of his youth, since he had extensive knowledge of the Qur'an, *hadith*, religion and the *Shari'a*, he could, much to the surprise of his audience, give excellent lectures. He would also criticise those who quoted weak *hadiths*. At his straight-forward and sharp criticism, several of the *'ulama'* became infuriated and they started a campaign against him. These opponents could not match him in the field of knowledge, but they matched him in the field of conspiracy. They succeeded in having him deported from Damascus on the grounds of his "blasphemous" beliefs.

He went to Makka in 1292 and performed the *hajj* and remained there and in Madina for some time. Then he went to Cairo and in 1299 he issued a *fatwa* on the qualities of Allah which infuriated the *'ulama'* again and contrived to get him expelled from Egypt. After this he lost his professorship in the Damascus University and was ousted from Damascus. He went to Cairo again and participated in a *jihad* against the Mongols. He was present at the defeat of the Mongols at Shak-hab near Damascus. Then he campaigned against the Isma'ilis, Nusayris and Hakimis who used to believe 'Ali to be infallible and the Prophet's Companions to be unbelievers, and who did not say prayers, nor fast and who considered pork to be *halal*.

In 1307 he went to Cairo with a Shafi'i *qadi* and faced charges in the court of the Sultan. The court consisted of jurists and *'ulama'* of all aspects of Islam. For five days the court was held and the charges of blasphemy against him and against two of his brothers were heard. The court decreed that he and his brothers should be imprisoned. For one and a half years he remained in prison. Then he was again tried for blasphemy for writing a book against the *Ittihadiya*, but in the trial his opponents could not match his sharp logic and apposite arguments. They had to release him. But shortly afterwards he was re-arrested and imprisoned for a year and a half. This time he started lecturing to the prisoners and engaged himself in the pursuit of knowledge.

Then he was put behind bars again in Alexandria and remained there for eight months. Then he was brought back to Cairo where Sultan an-Nasir wanted to help him by declaring his fight against his personal enemies to be a *jihad*. But Ibn Taymiyya flatly refused to let this be done. The Sultan, in any case, was greatly moved by his great qualities and appointed him a professor in his university.

In 1313 he was allowed to leave Cairo with a war expedition to Syria. After an absence of seven years and seven months, he was able to visit his birthplace, Damascus, where he was received with great honour and reinstated in his old post of professor. For five years he continued in this post undisturbed and wrote several books on Islam. In 1318 he issued a *fatwa* relating to *talaq* against the will of the Sultan and again fell into disfavour and was imprisoned in Damascus. He was released after five months.

Thereafter he dedicated himself to his studies and writings and to preaching his views on Islam. At this time, he issued several *fatwas* and sermons against Pir-worship and visits to tombs. At this his opponents influenced the Sultan against him and he was arrested in 1326 and interned in a cell in the citadel of Damascus. However, he was allowed a separate room in the prison to enable him to continue his studies and research. He occupied himself by writing a *tafsir* of the Qur'an and on other subjects of Islam. But unfortunately when his opponents came too know of this, they snatched away all his manuscripts, papers and even his pen. This was indeed the harshest deprivation which could be inflicted on him.

After this, he devoted his days and nights to reading

the Qur'an and to saying prayers and fasting. But the shock had a severe effect on him and he died within twenty days on 27th September, 1328. At his death, all of Damascus was plunged into grief. Two hundred thousand men and fifteen thousand women attended his funeral prayer.

Ibn Taymiyya was a dedicated, sincere and straightforward Muslim who was a true follower of the *Shari'a* and who did not approve of the introduction of the shaykh as an intermediary between man and his Lord, nor did he approve of people visiting graves. All of this he did in accordance with the *Shari'a* because the many Muslims in his time had become corrupted by unscrupulous *pirs* and by over-emphasis on visiting graves. The same disease has engulfed our society now. Many people in India, Pakistan and Bangladesh are now more busy with their Pirs than with Allah. And tomb visiting has become a fashion and a "cure" for all diseases.

Ibn Taymiyya, being an ardent follower of *tawhid*, could not tolerate any middle-man between Allah and man. There is room for such a man in Islam as a teacher, as a guide, as a helper and as a friend, but certainly not as a man to be worshipped. It is true that in his time pragmatists and supporters of pragmatism and argumentation were on the decline and the supporters of *taqlid* were on the rise. This gave rise to several *bid'as* (innovations) in Islam, and these innovations dented the beliefs and practices of the Muslims. And it is for this reason that several scholars, including Ibn Taymiyya, rose up against these innovations and asked people to follow the Qur'an and the Prophet strictly, and not to go near the *Pirs* or *Mazars*. He used to declare, "Only the

Almighty Allah is fit for our prayer," and, "Nobody else, no Prophet, no *pir*, no sufi, no religious leader, is fit for our prayer. And if anybody makes any supplication to any *pir* he becomes a *kafir*." This is quite in tune with the ideals of Islam.

Ibn Taymiyya was a dedicated, sincere and straightforward follower of Islam. His thoughts were clear, his obedience and submission to Allah were direct. His knowledge of the Qur'an and the *Sunna* was vast. He was against the Kharijites, Rafidites, Qadarites, Mu'tazilites and all such sects. He was for the Qur'an and sound *hadiths*, not for weak *hadiths*. It is said that he wrote more than five hundred books on the Qur'an and the *Sunna*, but most of them have been lost and only sixty-four are still available.

People used to respect him as he was an inspiring man with an inspirational character. Throughout his entire life, he fought against *Pirs* and Sufis, but *Pirs* and Sufis still exist in our society. But his teachings were not in vain. Four hundred years later, Muhammad ibn 'Abdu'l-Wahhab (1703-1787) put his teachings into practice in Saudi Arabia.

23
Ibn Khaldun (1332 - 1406)

Had it not been for a word that went forth before from your Lord, (their punishment) must necessarily have come but for a term appointed (for respite). (Qur'an 20:129)

The founder of the social sciences and the greatest Muslim historian, 'Abdu'r-Rahman Wali'ud-din Muhammad ibn Khaldun, was born in Tunisia on 27 May 1332. His forefathers had migrated from Hadramawt to Seville (in Spain) in the ninth century AD and were employed by their rulers as statesmen and administrators over almost four centuries. In the thirteenth century his family was one of the ruling families of Seville. Before the end of the century Seville had been occupied by the Christians, and his family had to emigrate to Tunis like most of the other noble families,

His father was a prominent scholar of Islam and so he received his primary education from his father and from other qualified and learned scholars of Islam. From his boyhood his sharp intelligence and philosophical ideas attracted attention. When he was twenty, he was appointed by the Sultan of Fes as his private secretary. But his philosophical ideas alienated the *'ulama'* class and he had to leave Fes. He then became private secretary to the Marinid Sultan, Abu 'Inan. Through his service, position and status at the court of the Sultan he became very rich and famous in a very short time, but he fell out of favour and ended up in prison.

He somehow managed to escape from prison and went to Granada to seek asylum under its Sultan, Muhammad.

There he was accepted with great honour by the famous historian and politician of Spain, Ibn al-Khatib (1313-74). Ibn al-Khatib was simultaneously a great historian, philosopher, geographer and poet. He wrote more than sixty books, twenty of which are still available. By courtesy of Ibn al-Khatib, Ibn Khaldun became a favourite of the Sultan who gave him the position of State Ambassador and sent him to King Pedro of Castille to draw up a special treaty with the King. King Pedro, seeing his political acumen and diplomatic expertise, asked him to become a Minister in his kingdom, but Ibn Khaldun politely refused the offer.

After having stayed two years in Granada, he went back to North Africa and was involved in solving several political problems and undertook various assignments in the states of North Africa over a period of about ten years from 1364 to 1374. However, despite his untiring efforts, he failed to bring about peace among the small African states and in the end decided to spend a solitary life in a fort in Oran. Here for four years he devoted himself with all his heart to researches on history, planned his seminal book of world history and wrote a part of the *Muqaddima* (Introduction) to it. To gather material for this book, he roamed from place to place, from library to library and from institution to institution. At last he went to the Zaytun University of Tunis in 1380 and stayed there to complete the writing of his famous *Muqaddima*.

After two years, he went to Egypt on his way to Makka to perform *hajj*. In Egypt, Sultan 'Ali Zahir (1382-1398) received him with great honour and appointed him as principal of the famous Al-Azhar University. After two years he was appointed the Chief Justice of the Maliki *madh-hab* court. As a justice, he introduced several improvements and amendments in Maliki law, but he had to face severe criticism from several quarters. His opponents even held a court of enquiry against him, but they could not establish any charge. At this time his family was shipwrecked and drowned at sea while coming from Tunis to Cairo. He lost all his children, wife and other relations, and this loss was a very cruel blow to him. He resigned from service and from the world and devoted himself to the worship of Allah. After three years he went to Makka to perform the *hajj* and then he returned to Cairo to dedicate himself to writing. By 1392 the writing of his famous World History was complete.

The later life of Ibn Khaldun is described in his autobiography which was published in Cairo. From this we find that Ibn Khaldun travelled to Damascus with the Mamluk Sultan in 1400 AD but out of fear of Timur-i-leng (Tamerlane), the Sultan fled back to Cairo. Ibn Khaldun met Timur, and, as a consummate statesman, very diplomatically persuaded him against invading Syria, Egypt and other Western countries. Timur liked Ibn Khaldun very much and offered him the post of Prime Minister and wanted to enter Egypt. But Ibn Khaldun dissuaded him from that very tactfully by saying that he preferred to live peacefully in his home alone rather than become the Prime Minister of Samarqand. Timur granted him his request and prevented his Mongol army from attacking Egypt.

The Mamluk Sultan of Egypt, out of gratitude to Ibn Khaldun, appointed him Chief Justice of all of Egypt. He died on 19 March 1406 at the age of seventy-four.

Ibn Khaldun became famous as the father of social science. His great book, *The History of the World,* particularly its *Muqaddima*, is not only a unique contribution to historical works, but a new chapter and illumination in the world of letters as a whole. His travels from Seville to Samarqand and his experience of administration and politics under different kings and sultans, his important diplomatic assignments to several countries, and above all his persuasive qualities demonstrated by deterring the Tartar Timur from launching an invasion which would have meant the almost certain destruction of Egypt, Syria and other countries, speak of his great personality, acumen and keen intelligence.

His practical experience and his vast learning combined together to give the world a book which became an inspiration to all historians and writers of the world. This book is called *Kitab al-'Ibar*. It is divided into three parts, the first is the *Muqaddima*, which can be called the origin of all the social sciences. From this point of view, he is the predecessor of all later social scientists, and certainly of the English social scientist, Toynbee, who wrote the *A Study of History* five hundred years later.

It is Ibn Khaldun who brought about the changes in the attitude of men towards history, towards rulers, towards the ruled, towards their God. He declared that the state and civilization run according to certain basic rules and these basic rules apply to all people, irrespective of their creed, colour or climate. Ibn Khaldun said that history was not only the story of nations and religions. History is the narration of all man's activities. It is the story of the development of human civilization. A historian's role is to record man's day-to-day problems and changes.

The fundamental discovery of the gradual

development of human society and judging all events of history according to that discovery is the philosophy of history that Ibn Khaldun propounded. And according to Toynbee this was the greatest contribution of Ibn Khaldun.

In the world of economics, knowledge and science he had unprecedented influence. He used to place belief above philosophy. What is not understood by naked reasoning or argumentation is sure to be understood by belief in Allah and in the Hereafter. He discussed this point in great length in one of his original essays, and something of this has also been discussed in his *Muqaddima*.

When evaluating Ibn Khaldun we must remember that, while sitting in a palace in North Africa five hundred years ago, he contributed to the world of history and to the world as a whole a knowledge and a direction upon which all later historians based themselves. So he is, in truth, the father of the science of history.

24
Jalalu'd-din as-Suyuti (1445 - 1505)

Every soul shall taste death. In the end, to Us shall you be brought back. (Qur'an 29:57)

In Egypt during the reign of the Mamluk Sultans of all those heroes and scholars of Islam who emerged, the historian, Jalalu'd-din as-Suyuti, is the most famous. Undoubtedly he was one of the greatest scholars and thinkers of the fifteenth century.

He was born in Upper Egypt in 1445 AD in a place called Asyut from which he took his surname of as-Suyuti. He lost his father early in life but he was left financially independent and so he faced no difficulty in pursuing his studies.

His memory was very retentive. At the age of eight he became a *hafiz* of the Qur'an. His mother, being a very intelligent lady, arranged for his education with all the best contemporary scholars. He learnt *tafsir, hadith, fiqh, 'ilm al-Kalam,* history, philosophy, philology and rhetoric under them.

After having finished his studies he went to the university in Cairo and became a professor of several subjects, one after another. Since he was well schooled in almost all the subjects, he soon became the head of the professors. In 1501 his opponents conspired to implicate him in the misappropriation of university funds and he resigned out of regret. He devoted the rest of his life to studies and writings and to the worship of Allah. He selected a lonely place on the island of Rawda in the Nile and dedicated himself to writing his celebrated books and here he died after four years in the year 1505.

Jalalu'd-din was a great genius and a great scholar. He continued throughout his life to write extensively on the Qur'an, *hadith*, Shari'a, history, philosophy, rhetoric, etc, and contributed a great deal to the world of knowledge. It is said that his books number more than five hundred.

As-Suyuti concentrated on the demands of his readers. He had the capacity to write books on subjects which would attract the reader and he is famous throughout the Muslim world for writing excellent and attractive books. His books continue to be read with interest in Egypt, Morocco, Syria, and even in the Indian sub-continent. It is undoubtedly true that it was he who presented Muslim history and culture to his readers in a scientific way and in an accessible, enjoyable manner. In this way, his contribution to the Muslim reading public throughout the world has been tremendous and most effective. His most popular and acclaimed books are *Al-Itiqan fi 'ulum al-Qur'an*, a book about the Holy Qur'an. *Tafsir al-Jalalayn* written partly by Jalalu'd-din al-Mahalli and the rest by himself, *Muzhir al-Lugha, Husn al-Muhadara Misr wa'l-Qahira,* and *Tarikh al-Khulafa'*.

Tafsir al-Jalalayn is a very famous *tafsir* and it is very popular throughout the whole of the Islamic world. It is very simple and lucid and dependable. The *Misr wa'l-Qahira* is a voluminous book on the history of Egypt and it is very popular among Egyptian readers. The *Tarikh al-Khulafa'* is another very interesting book and is very popular among scholars and general readers.

All these books and writings indicate his unusual talent and foresight as a writer, as a reformer and as a keen observer. His wonderful and skilful writing, his faultless narration and his lucid language have endeared him to generations of readers, and for centuries it has been the great and enlightening as-Suyuti whose writings have inspired the Muslims.

25
Shah Waliullah (1703 - 1762)

Those who reject faith and do wrong, Allah will not forgive them nor guide them to any way.
(Qur'an 4:168)

At the beginning of the eighteenth century, the Mughal empire began to decline. On the one hand, the Sikhs, the Marathas, etc. were asserting themselves and, on the other, the provinces were declaring independence from their allegiance to Delhi. In the social and religious life of the Muslims, all sorts of injustice and indiscipline were prevailing. Seeing all this, the conscientious people of Muslim society were perturbed and they started awakening Muslim society by instilling in them the finer values of Islam through Islamic education and through political uprisings.

This two-pronged movement had as its aims the overthrow of the growing power of the Sikhs, the Marathas and the English rulers, and the inspiration of the Muslim masses by giving them the true knowledge of the Qur'an and *Sunnah* which would enable them to remember their lost heritage and return to their culture and tradition. The leader of this movement was Shaykh al-Hind Mawlana Shah Waliullah.

Mawlana Shah Waliullah was born in Delhi in 1703 to a noble Muslim family of sufis and scholars. According to many people, he was a descendent of the Mujaddid Alf-i-Sani Shaykh Ahmad Sirhindi. Many genuises were born to this family who were great Sufis and *'ulama'* and who left their influence on the Islamic ways of life among the Muslims of India. His grandfather, Shah Wajihuddin, was an advisor to Alamgir Awrangzeb and his father, Shah 'Abdu'r-Rahim helped Alamgir in editing the *Fatwa-i-Alamgiri*.

He was a man of genius. In his boyhood he studied with his father and then with many other scholars of Delhi. He studied Arabic and Persian literature, *tafsir* of the Qur'an, *hadith, fiqh*, and usul. Then he studied Muslim *'aqa'id*, Islamic history, philosophy, law and logic. He also had great interest in social science and studied Ibn Khaldun's World History as well as versing himself in politics. This is why, although he was a great scholar and a great orthodox *'alim*, his writings betray an acute analytical power and sharp insight into the political problems of India and the Muslim world.

At the age of 16 or 17 he became a *muhaddith* in the Rahimiya Madrasa established by his father. He turned the *madrasa* into an ideal institution by his dedicated teaching and reformed education system. Then he left for *hajj* and studied in Makka under Shah Abu Tahir, a reputed *'alim* of Makka. After his return from Makka in 1730 at the age of twenty-seven, he started teaching again.

His son, Shams al-Hind, Mawlana 'Abdu'l-'Aziz, and his grandson, Shah Isma'il Shahid, and Mawlana 'Abdu'l-'Aziz's son-in-law, Mawlana 'Abdu'l-Hayy, were directly inspired by his teachings and thoughts. Of them, Shah Isma'il Shahid (1777-1831) is the most famous. Dr. Allama Iqbal once remarked about him, "India has so far produced one really great *'alim* and his name is Isma'il. He did not spend his life reading books and giving *fatwas*, he sacrificed his life for Islam and for recovering the lost heritage of Islam by declaring *jihad* against the infidels. It is undoubtedly true that Shah Waliullah's books and writings inspired the Muslims of India to the spirit of *jihad* which was led by Shah Isma'il Shahid."

Shah Waliullah was a very mild, gentle and independent thinker. His lack of self-seekingwas uncommon. He lived all his life in Delhi near the Mughal emperors but he never went near the Mughal courts for fame or worldly benefits. Even so his daily audience and followers who came to seek his spiritual favours numbered thousands and included kings, nobles, Sufis, *'ulama'* and beggars. But he did not care for any earthly fame or earthly benefits or wealth, and he devoted himself to giving spiritual instruction to his devotees and to worshipping Allah.

In 1737 he translated the Qur'an into Persian for the first time in India. For this the *'ulama'* of Delhi campaigned against him and he had to leave Delhi for some time. Also his son, 'Abdu'l-Qadir, translated the Qur'an into Urdu for the first time in India. Based on this Urdu translation of the Qur'an of 1885 by 'Abdu'l-Qadir, Girish Chandra Sen of Bengal translated the Qur'an into Bengali for the first time.

But Shah Waliullah was not oblivious of the contemporary political situation that was unfolding all around him. The Mughals were losing their royal grip rapidly, the Marathas, the Sikhs, etc. were on the rise, the British and the French were gaining in strength - all these forces were making him unsettled. He was particularly mortified at seeing the Muslims' downfall politically, religiously and socially, and so he gave fiery speeches and inspiring lectures to incite them to *jihad* as a self-respecting nation. Two of his important books on this, *Fuyuz al-Haramayn* and *Tafhima al-Ilahiya* are vivid examples of his genuine concern for the Muslims' welfare.

It was his fiery ideas that took effect later, when a class of Muslim reformers emerged in India to remind and inspire the Muslims to fight against all evils. He shared the concern of one the Wahhabis of the Arabian peninsula in rooting out all *bid'a* and Hindu customs that had crept in among the Muslims. At that time there was no other man like him, able to call people to Islam by giving the correct *tafsir* of the Qur'an and interpreting the *hadith* correctly. He gave the true explanation of *jihad* and inspired the Muslims all over India to fight against evil and against oppressors.

By doing this he was, on the one hand, making the Muslims aware of the causes of their downfall in order to help them restore their position, and on the other, he was preparing the Muslims of the Indian sub-continent for a true *jihad* to establish an Islamic government in India. In fact, it was Shah Waliullah who first sowed the seeds of Islamic nationhood among the Muslims of India and it was he who inspired them to fight *jihad* to establish their rights.

26
Jamalu'd-din Al-Afghani (1839 - 1897)

Is then He Who creates like the one that does not create? Will you not receive admonition? (Qur'an 16:17)

In the eighteenth century, the entire Muslim world languished in the darkness of a barren period. There was no emergence of a great *Mujaddid* in this period. From the end of the eighteenth to date there have been several *mujaddids* (reformers). There was reawakening among the Muslims in Arabia, in West Africa, Sudan, Egypt, Syria, Iran, Afghanistan and even in the Indian sub-continent.

This reawakening was again due to the emergence of a few *mujaddids* in the eighteenth and ninteeth centuries who were responsible for initiating the tide of a new movement in the life of the Muslims in the religious, social, political and economic spheres. The hero of this Renaissance is the fiery leader Sayyid Jamalu'd-din al-Afghani. Al-Afghani was born in a place called Asad-Abad near Kabul in 1839. His father Sayyid Safdar was a descendant of the famous *muhaddith*, Abu Musa at-Tirmidhi (823-893), who was a descendant of Imam Husayn.

Sayyid Jamalu'd-din had his early education until the age of ten in his local *madrasa* and then he went to a senior *madrasa* in Kabul where he studied for another five years, and then he studied in several *madrasas* of Iran until the age of eighteen. In these *madrasas* he studied Arabic literature, Arabic grammar, history, *hadith, tafsir, fiqh, usul,* law, *mantiq,* philosophy, Sufism, revelation, mathematics, natural science and medicine. After the age of eighteen. he came to India where he studied English, French, European philosophy and science.

His brain was very sharp and his memory was very fertile. He could learn any subject very easily with little effort. He was well-versed in the Afghan language, in French, Arabic, English, Turkish and Persian. In 1857, he left for *hajj* and came into contact with several famous *'ulama'* of Makka and Madina.

After his return from Makka, he accepted a job under Sultan Amir Dost of Afghanistan. In 1864, when Amir Dost died, there was a clash among his brothers about who should succeed the throne. Jamalu'd-din sided with one brother, Muhammad Azam, who ultimately won and made him his prime minister. He was at that time only 27. But after a while Azam's other brother, Sher 'Ali, defeated him , and with the connivance of the British, ascended the throne. Sher 'Ali retained Jamalu'd-din as prime minister for some time, but was inwardly conspiring to get him killed. Jamalu'd-din scented the conspiracy and left for India on the pretext of making the *hajj*. But here also he was to remain under the surveillance of the British, and so after one month, he left for Cairo where he started lecturing in the Al-Azhar University.

From Cairo he went to Istanbul (in 1870) and Sultan 'Abdu'l-Hamid received him with great honour. His fiery speeches and revolutionary ideas moved the intelligentsia and the university students alike. He was able to create a stir in the city. But the orthodox *'ulama'* got furious because of his revolutionary ideas and the Shaykh of the *'ulama'* of Istanbul became his enemy. The Shaykh was further infuriated by a revolutionary speech he made in a Turkish University, and the *'ulama'* demanded his expulsion from Turkey so vehemently that the Sultanate was obliged to expel him from Turkey.

He returned to Cairo and was received with great honour by the Prime Minister, Riyaz Pasha, who granted him a monthly stipend. He decided to stay in Cairo and then turned towards reforming the social, political and religious affairs of the Egyptians. Students and the intelligentsia started gathering in his house and he started giving them progressive lectures on Islamic theology and Sufism. At the time Egypt's main sources of revenue were being usurped, one after the other, by the British and the French, because of the inefficient policies and administration indulged in by Isma'il Pasha. Jamalu'd-din started criticising the British and the French for their interference in Egypt's internal affairs and began inciting the youth against them.

At this juncture, Mufti Muhammad 'Abduh became a close disciple of his and he created a reawakening among the Egyptians with new and revolutionary ideas. Jamalu'd-din and Muhammad 'Abduh campaigned with untiring efforts for nearly eight years and succeeded in initiating a new awakening among the Egyptians and a change in their religious and social attitudes. Simultaneously their political life was also changed and the people of Egypt began to accept his ideas and reforms in their overall attitude to life. .

In 1879, Tawfiq Pasha became a pawn in the hands of the British and he expelled Jamalu'd-din from Egypt. Jamalu'd-din came back to India and wrote his famous book *Reply to the Materialists* in French. In 1182, there was further upheaval in Egypt under the leadership of Arabi Pasha and the British seized the opportunity to occupy Egypt. Jamalu'd-din stayed in India under virtual house arrest, but after some time, was eventually allowed to leave for London. From London he went to Paris where he stayed for three years. During this period he began to criticise, through the French newspapers, the role of the European Imperialists in subjugating and exploiting the Muslim countries. In 1884, Muhammad 'Abduh also joined him in Paris after having been expelled from Egypt, and both of them co-operated in publishing a newspaper in Arabic from Paris called *Al-'Urwah Al-Wuthqa*. Through this paper they strongly criticised the British for their exploitation of the Muslims and they called for Muslim unity.

After this, he left for London and then for Russia. He stayed in Russia for four years and continued his political propagation very strongly through the columns of their newspapers. In 1189 he met the Shah of Iran, Shah Nasir'ud-din, who appointed him as his Prime Minister. But in a few years he had differences with the Shah and had to leave Iran for Basra and then for London in 1891. In 1892 he came to Constantinople and Sultan 'Abdul-Hamid received him with honour. But soon the Sultan also became hostile to him and he had to live under house arrest. During this period, he had nobody by his side except his Christian servant to look after him. He died in the lap of this Christian servant on 9 May 1897 after suffering for quite some time from cancer. After his death he was, of course, buried with great fanfare and honour in the graveyard of the Shaykhs of Constantinople.

In modern history Jamalu'd-din al-Afghani is considered as one of the greatest fighters for Muslim independence. His field of operations was the entire world. His dream was to inspire the Muslims all over the world to rediscover themselves, to wake up, to reassert themselves, and to unite in the fight against the exploitation of Western imperialists. Afghanistan, Iran, Turkey, Egypt, and the sub-continent were his main fields of activity. The revolution of Iran (of those days) was done according to his plan, the reawakening of modern Egypt was his planning, and the nationalist revolutions in most other countries were carried out under his inspiration including the 1908 revolution of the Young Turks in Turkey.

He was a fearless man, undaunted in spirit, a great personality, of sharp intelligence, revolutionary thought, unparalleled oratory, far-reaching foresight - all these qualities combined to make him one of the greatest thinkers of history. He believed that the Muslim world should come under one Khalif, and only then would they be able to wipe out the influence and rule of European nations over them. With this strong belief in his heart he formed the *Umm al-Qura'*, a pan-Islamic organisation to bring all Muslims under its flag. He is the father of "Pan-Islamicism". The present Mu'tamar al-'Alam al-Islami and the Rabita 'Alam al-Islami are rooted in his pan-Islamic movement. The first session of the Mu'tamar al-'Alam was held in 1898, one year after his death.

For his far-sighted views and international ideas, Allama Iqbal called him "a living link between the past and the present" and observed, "Had his untiring efforts been spent with the only goal of establishing Islam as a humanitarian and active religion, the Muslim world would have benefited more."

His principal achievement was to present Islam as a progressive religion vis-`a-vis scientific research and analysis. He gave a new direction to the progressive aspects of Islam in the light of modern ideas and scientific inquiries. And here he came into conflict with the orthodox *'ulama'* class who would not brook his progressive ideas.

Prof. E.G. Browne, the expert on Persian history and literature tells us about him:

> Jamalu'd-din was a man of excellent character, of great scholarship, of unusual genius, of undaunted spirit, of tremendous energy and of unsurpassed oratory. He was simultaneously a philosopher, a thinker, an orator, a journalist and above all, a top politician, whom people used to regard as a great patriot and the rulers as a great revolutionary.

To end with, a few words from his book, *Reply to the Materialists* which was also later translated by his disciple Muhammad 'Abduh into Arabic:

> Every nation must have a class of people who will give them the light of education, and another class who will give them the regulations of morality. One class will remove their ignorance and will give them the light of education, and the other class will give them the moral education to prevent them from perversion.

27
Allama Shibli Nomani (1857-1964)

The balance that Day will be true. Those whose scale of good will be heavy will prosper. (Qur'an 7:8)

In 1857 the Indian Muslims and freedom-loving sepoys had launched the Sepoy Mutiny, and had encircled the district jail of Azamgarh. At this critical point in time Allama Shibli Nomani was born into a noble family of Azamgarh, the Rawat descendent of a Rajpat family. His father, Habibullah, an advocate of the civil court and also a trader in indigo, arranged for his son to study with several *'ulama'* of Azamgarh to teach him good Arabic, Persian, *tafsir, hadith* and *fiqh*. He also studied Muslim theology and law, and attained good knowledge in history, philosophy and poetry.

Shibli by his mother's side was a descendents of Imam Abu Hanifa an-Noman and hence he was called Nomani. During his time the prestige of the Urdu language was increasing as most of the rising stars of India were adopting Urdu in place of Persian (because of British intervention and influence), and so he learnt and mastered Urdu very well. Another reason that Urdu became more popular was because of Ghalib who was an excellent Urdu poet and whose name and fame spread far and wide.

In fact, in northern India, during his time it was Urdu which flourished and which was accepted by most Muslims and Hindus as the literary language of the people. It is not an exaggeration to say that after Shams al-Hind, Mawlana Shah 'Abdu'l-'Aziz, it was Allama Shibli Nomani who started teaching and writing on Islam through Urdu and who accepted Urdu as his vehicle of expression.

By the age of nineteen he walready a well-known *'alim* and he went to Makka to do *hajj* and there he devoted his time to fuering his studies inMuslim theology, history, philosophy and Sufism from different *'ulama'* of Arabia. He was a staunch supporter of the *Shari'a* and was an orthodox Hanafi Muslim. He was a determined opponent of the Wahhabi movement who were spreading their ultra-reforms in the name of the *Shari'a*. By his resistance, he earned a good name among the orthodox Muslims of India.

When he returned to India from Makka, he found Sir Syed Ahmed (1817-1898) was already well-advanced with his programme of introducing western education and culture through the English language among the Muslim students of India. Syed Ahmed was dedicating his whole time and energy to inspire the Muslims to change their outlook and to accept western education and culture. For this purpose, he had established the famous Aligarh University and asked Muslim students all over India to take up Western education and the English language.

Shibli, although he was an orthodox Muslim, was greatly attracted to the alluring programme of Sir Syed Ahmed and he liked his educational reforms and certain aspects of his cultural revolution. One day he went to the Aligarh University to get his younger brother admitted there and by a matter of chance he saw Sir Syed Ahmed who requested him to take up a professorship in his university and he accepted it. He taught in Aligarh for sixteen years and there he came in contact with Thomas Arnold and several other English scholars from whom he got acquainted with modern Western ideas and thoughts. He also travelled with Thomas Arnold in 1892 to Syria, Egypt, Turkey and to some other Muslim countries of the Middle East and got direct and practical experience of their religious, social and political life and problems. His deep scholarship influenced Thomas Arnold on one hand and on the other he was influenced by Arnold to a great extent, and through this there was a modern touch in his ideas and thoughts owing to his contact with Western scholars.

After the death of Sir Syed Ahmed he left Aligarh and became an advisor in the Education Department of Hyderabad State. He initiated many reforms and changes in their education system. From his policy, the Usmania University of Hyderabad adopted Urdu as the medium of instruction. Before that no other university of India adopted any vernacular language as the medium of instruction in higher studies. In 1908 he left Hyderabad and went to Lucknow to become the principal of the famous Jami'a Nadwa al-'Ulum there. He stayed there for five years and introduced several reforms in its teaching and curriculum and injected some modern methods in its educational system. At this the orthodox class of *'ulama'* became hostile to him and he had to leave Lucknow for his birthplace, Azamgarh, in 1913.

Here in Azamgarh he established an Islamic academy called the Dar al-Musannifin, or the House of Writers. Until the last days of his life he dedicated himself to the development of this academy. In the later years of his life it became a high class research academy and was named the Shibli Academy. Several renowned professors and *'ulama'* of India spent time at this Research Academy and benefited. In 1914 Allama Shibli Nomani died in

Azamgarh.

Shibli was a profound and versatile scholar in Arabic, Persian and Urdu. He was also a versatile poet and in his early life he wrote many poems in Urdu and Arabic. But his genius found its real expression in the Urdu language and literature and he is remembered now as a great writer of Urdu.

Towards the end of the nineteenth century, there emerged a few Muslim thinkers in India who wanted to give modern light to the Muslims of India after having inspired them with the heritage of the Muslim past. These influential thinkers were the torch-bearers of the century, and the Renaissance that they were able to give birth to included personalities like Sir Syed Ahmed in leadership, and Altaf Husayn Hali, Shibli Nomani and Dr. Allama Iqbal in scholarship. Hali's poems and Shibli's books and articles were able to regenerate the Muslims of the subcontinent to aspire for their lost heritage. And Iqbal's fiery speeches and fiery poems and *ghazals* gave them a new direction in life and made them boast of their traditions. In this way Shibli's contribution to the reawakening and rebirth of the Muslim nationhood is indeed great.

Shibli's genius had its flowering when he was a professor in Aligarh University for sixteen years when he came into contact with Sir Syed Ahmed and British scholars in Aligarh. But Shibli and Sir Syed were poles apart. Sir Syed Ahmed wanted to adapt Islam to Western thinking and style, while Shibli wanted to adapt Western thinking and style to Islam. But both wanted the good and welfare of the Muslims. Sir Syed wanted to save the Muslims from the wrath of the British rulers after their active participation in the Sepoy Mutiny and other anti-

British acts. Shibli wanted to save the Muslims from their ruination by making them self-reliant and self-respecting by regaining their lost heritage and tradition. He never bowed to Western power and influence, although he had many Western friends and admirers. In other words, Shibli was never a lover of Western philosophy and culture, whereas Sir Syed was.

Shibli was a great supporter of Pan-Islamism. He wrote several poems and articles decrying the British and other Western powers when Turkey was defeated in the Balkan war, and he urged the world Muslims to unite. In 1913, when the British Administration in India stormed the Cawnpur Mosque, Shibli stood against the British and wrote many poems condemning them for which he was also harassed and humiliated.

Shibli was well aware of the progress of science and education in the West. He wanted to inspire the Muslims to make similar progress by having recourse to their lost heritage and culture, and warned them against getting lost in Western culture. In keeping with this goal, he wrote his famous books, *As-Sirat al-Numan, al-Faruq, al-Ma'mun, Al-Ghazzali, Mawlana Rumi* and the immortal *Sirat an-Nabi*. This last book, *Sirat an-Nabi*, is a unique book on the life of the Prophet and is acclaimed as one of the best books in the world. He wrote only four volumes of this book and the remaining four volumes were written by his disciple, Syed Sulaiman Nadvi.

Shibli was a great and keen observer and an acute critic. In fact, he was the first critic of the Urdu language and literature. His great book *Shayer al-Azam* written in five volumes, giving a critical analysis of Persian poets and Persian poetry, is a scholastic book of high calibre. His two others books, *Muqalat-i Shibli* and *Rasa'il-i Shibli*, are also very important critical books.

Shibli's language was very clear and simple, his narration very alive and attractive, his arguments very scholarly and his devotion to Islam genuine.

28
Dr Allama Mohammad Iqbal (1873 - 1938)

Glory to Him! He is high above all that they say. Exalted and Great (beyond measure)! (Qur'an 17:43)

The whole nineteenth century was passing through a period of turmoil for the millions of Muslims of the Indian sub-continent. Their political and cultural arena was disturbed, but they were fortunate enough to have been graced by the birth of several geniuses who left their mark and influence on their lives. Dr. Allama Mohammad Iqbal was one of the leaders of these luminaries.

He was born on 22 February 1873 in Sialkot, Punjab. His forefathers were Kashmiri Brahmims who accepted Islam, possibly in the seventeenth century. His father, Nur Muhammad, was a pious Muslim who resigned from government service and started doing business. He sent his eldest son, 'Ata' Muhammad, to a *madrasa,* and sent the youngest son, Iqbal, to a missionary school. Here in the mission school he met a famous and good *'alim,* Mir Hasan, who inspired Iqbal to study Islam.

From Sialkot he went to the Government College, Lahore, for higher studies, and in 1899 he did his M.A. in Philosophy at this college. Thereafter he taught as a professor in the Oriental College and then in the Government College, Lahore, for six years. During this period he came into contact with the famous orientalist, Thomas Arnold, and became very friendly with him. While he was greatly influenced by Mir Hasan in his Islamic studies and thoughts, he was equally greatly influenced by Thomas Arnold in his Western ideas and thoughts. It was Thomas Arnold who influenced him to go for higher studies in England in 1905.

He devoted three years to his studies in Europe. He studied Philosophy at Cambridge University with the famous philosopher, James Ward, and others and then he did a PhD in Persian mysticism at Munich University in Germany. Then he passed the Bar-at-Law in England and taught as a professor of Arabic at London University for six months.

In 1908, when he was thirty-five, Dr. Mohammad Iqbal returned to Lahore and started as a professor of English and Philosophy in the Government College there, and simultaneously started practising law in the Punjab High Court. After three years, he resigned from Government service and devoted himself to practising law. When he resigned from Government service he told his life-long friend, Khadim 'Ali Bakhsh, "I want to give something to my nation, but this Government slavery is a big obstacle. Now after my release from Government service, I can dedicate my life to achieving my goal."

Thereafter he dedicated himself completely to poetry and verse composition. He would devote only a few hours to his law practice and the rest of the time to his writing. He was never a very wealthy man. He earned just enough to live a modest life. But he was not able to afford to publicise his work abroad and that is why he was not favoured with any international award because he had no chance to present his immortal poems in any international forum.

In 1915 Iqbal wrote *Asrar-i-Khudi.*, in 1917*Rumz-i-Bekhudi*, in 1923 *Payam-i-Mashriq*, in 1924 *Bang-i-Dera*, and in 1927 *Jabur-i-Azam*. During this turbulent period many political upheavals were taking place in the Indian sub-continent and he could not remain isolated from the flow of these events. He jumped into them. In 1927 he became a Member of the Punjab Legislative Assembly and joined in active politics, voicing his fearless criticism of British rule. His advocacy for the rights of the people drew the attention of all.

In 1930, he was elected President of the Muslim League and he gave a fiery presidential speech at the Allahabad Conference of the League which was significant for many reasons. In this speech he gave a few original guidelines which were directed at the breaking of the political stalemate in India, and which gave an indication of a sovereign and independent Pakistan. Seven years later, on 20 June 1937, in a letter which he wrote to the Qa'id-i-Azam, Mohammad Ali Jinnah, he indicated the formation of a state comprising those provinces where Muslims were in the majority. Ten years later his prophecy came true and Pakistan was created, although he died in April, 1938, of heart failure.

In 1931 and 1932, he attended the Round Table Conference in London. In the 1932 Muslim League Conference he delivered a moving speech which showed his deep political foresight:

> Nationalism as defined and believed in by Europe is not what I believe in. If this kind of nationalism is imported into India the Muslims will not benefit. I oppose it, seeing it as Godless materialism, and this is what I believe to be the principal enemy of modern humanitarianism. . . What is most important is that a man lives on religion, culture and his tradition. He dies for these, and he lives for these, but certainly not for a

land where he is accidentally born.

In 1924 he suffered a chest pain, which later, in 1934, developed into serious throat trouble, as a result of which he lost his voice. In 1934, he was invited by Oxford University to speak on Rhodes, but for health reasons he had to decline the invitation. In 1937 he had a cataract in his eyes. He also had heart trouble and suffered from asthma. He died on 20 April 1938. Before he died, he wrote his last few lines of verse :

> A believer (in Allah), what is his sign?
> Listen: he accepts death with a smile.
> . . . .
> The life of this fakir is at its end here,
> Another fakir may or may not come here.

Iqbal was a very simple and plain man. He had no demands nor had he any wants. He was always surrounded by guests who were heartily entertained. He used to smoke from a hookah. He was a very pious Muslim. He was assiduous about doing the prayer and fasting during Ramadan. He had an unusual interest in reading the Qur'an and listening to it being recited and his eyes filled with tears when he heard it. He not only understood the Qur'an deeply but he was also an ardent believer in its every word.

His whole philosophy of life was dictated by the Qur'anic teachings and the *hadith* of the Prophet. He was a keen advocate of the Qur'an and *Sunna* as the main source of our strength. He was undoubtedly a great poet of Islam, a great forerunner of Islamic revival, and a great thinker of modern Islamic reformation. All his writing is full of Islamic ideals and Islamic glory and the beauty of Islam. He was all for the Islamic heritage and Islam's glorious past.

His two famous poems or mini-epics, *Shikwa* and *Jawab-i-Shikwa,* are full of reminiscence about the Muslim heritage and of the causes of their downfall. He complained to Allah about the sad state and downfall of the Muslims in *Shikwa,* and then in the *Jawab,* he pointed out the causes and reasons why they were deprived and asked why they should accept it as their destiny. In other words, they must come forward and they must assert themselves. He said,

> There is no one among you to seek for a houri from heaven;
> The mountain of Tur is there in Sinai, but there is no Musa to ask for it.

While he was in Europe for studies he observed three important things there which left a lasting impression on his mind: (i) the endless vitality of the Europeans, their unusual work-spirit and limitless inquisitiveness; (ii) the immense possibilities of human life whose practical results were being enjoyed and (iii) despite all these qualities and successes, they were in the grip of the curse of a hated class struggle and heartless competition. As a result all these achievements are not utilised for their welfare, and their downfall is concealed in their so-called success.

Seeing the failure of Western civilisation and its causes Dr. Iqbal, enlightened by the light of the Qur'an and *Sunna,* and enriched by the modern knowledge of the East and West, was able to give direction to the misguided Muslims in his famous speeches, *Reconstruction of Religious Thoughts in Islam*. The main theme behind all these speeches, and also behind all his writings and poetry, was to inspire the Muslims to rise up again and to reconstruct their glorious past in the light of the modern ideas and achievements.

To sum up, he was a modern Rumi, but he was not influenced by Rumi. He glowed by his own light and genius. He was indeed a great thinker and reformer.